Saturday's Child

Marie-Louise von Franz, Honorary Patron

**Studies in Jungian Psychology
by Jungian Analysts**

Daryl Sharp, General Editor

SATURDAY'S CHILD

Encounters
with the
Dark Gods

Janet O. Dallett

Also by Janet O. Dallett in this series:
When the Spirits Come Back (title 33, 1988)

Canadian Cataloguing in Publication Data

Dallett, Janet O. (Osborn), 1933-
    Saturday's child: encounters with the dark gods

(Studies in Jungian psychology by Jungian analysts; 51)

Includes bibliographical references.

ISBN 0-919123-52-X

1. Shadow (Psychoanalysis).
2. Good and evil—psychological aspects.
3. Jung, C.G. (Carl Gustav), 1875-1961—Religion.
I. Title. II. Series.

BF175.5.S55D35 1991   150.19'54   C91-093310-3

INNER CITY BOOKS
Box 1271, Station Q, Toronto, Canada M4T 2P4
Telephone (416) 927-0355
FAX 416-924-1814

Honorary Patron: Marie-Louise von Franz.
Publisher and General Editor: Daryl Sharp.
Senior Editor: Victoria Cowan.

INNER CITY BOOKS was founded in 1980 to promote the
understanding and practical application of the work of C.G. Jung.

Cover: Talisman Suite III (22" x 30"), etching/aquatint on Rives BFK
white, mounted on debossed Rives BFK grey (© Craig Antrim, 1982).

Printed and bound in Canada by John Deyell Company

Contents

See final page for descriptions of other Inner City Books

Acknowledgments

Thanks go first to my closest friend and *frater mysticus* in our mutual alchemy, my husband, known in these pages as Sean. He has lived the inner meaning of the book and many of its outer events along with me. If that were not enough, his devotion to his own writing and loving support of mine have been father and mother to my work.

Edward F. Edinger has been an inspiration to me, as analyst, writer and human being. His loyalty to Jung's vision and his own, especially regarding the shocking reality of divine incarnation in the human psyche, has given me courage to speak of my experience of that process and the dark side that predominates when it remains unconscious.

I am also grateful to the patients, colleagues and friends whose lives, along with mine, are knit into the fabric of the text; and the members of the Writers' Group, without whose patient and discerning comments, week by week, I would be lost.

To Lilith and Wotan, for whose sake I have been obliged to write this book. I ask them to bless it, and pray that it will serve their ultimate redemption.

The darkness drops again; but now I know
That twenty centuries of stony sleep
Were vexed to nightmare by a rocking cradle,
And what rough beast, its hour come round at last,
Slouches towards Bethlehem to be born?
—William Butler Yeats, "The Second Coming."

The view that good and evil are spiritual forces outside us, and that
man is caught in the conflict between them, is more bearable by
far than the insight that the opposites are the ineradicable and
indispensable preconditions of all psychic life, so much so that
life itself is guilt.
—C. G. Jung, *Mysterium Coniunctionis.*

God has fallen out of containment in religion and into the
unconscious of man, i.e., he is incarnating. Our unconscious is in
an uproar with the God who wants to know and to be known.
—Edward F. Edinger, *The Creation of Consciousness.*

Preface

William Blake's "Tiger! tiger! burning bright," with its enigmatic question, "Did he who made the lamb make thee?" has long been dear to me, for a tiger whose majesty I only later learned to cherish chased me round and round my earliest and recurrent childhood dream.

The beast that raged in our house also pursued my mother, in the form of an abiding fear that the house would burn down and the fantasy, every December, that the Christmas tree was going to catch on fire. With hindsight I see that both fire and tiger were rooted in the emotions that seethed unconsciously beneath our family's oh-so-proper surface. On a deeper level, my mother intuited that her polite, Sunday religion could burst into life and give birth to the very Christ who said "Whoever is near to me is near to the fire." Although my mother was not destined to meet a burning bush, she feared the possibility with good reason. To fall into the hands of the living God is a terrible thing indeed.

Fire and tiger have made this a hard book to write, and I have been tempted many times over to abandon the project. Right off the bat I came up against a distressing suspicion and an equally uncomfortable question. The suspicion was that in the world today the problem of evil and the problem of God incarnating in the human psyche are so closely intertwined as to be indistinguishable. The question: What, if anything, makes me different from the worst criminal?

As I wrote, I gradually came to understand that human feeling, ethical sensitivity, and the ability to contain and reflect truthfully upon our darkest selves can prevent the Satanic aspect of the godhead from having its way, and perhaps even transform it. I saw, too, that my willingness to crucify myself on dark impulses and emotions distinguishes me from the criminal, who merely acts on them. Jung has said these things repeatedly in many different ways,

11

but I have had to reinvent them from my own experience.

While working on the last chapter, I became blocked and could not go on. Then my husband and I exploded into an argument. It was a quarrel of the sort I had been writing about, all the while congratulating myself that we no longer had them. The next morning I awoke angry. Anger is no stranger to me, but this was a level of rage I had never known before. Cosmic. Murderous. I thought the top of my head was going to blow off. I do not like to see myself as someone who can feel that way.

It was a terrible experience, but without it, I would not have had the insight required to finish the chapter. What more can I say? I give fair warning. This book was born of many tigers.

1
What Rough Beast?

The coming new age will be as vastly different from ours as the
world of the 19th century was from that of the 20th with its atomic
physics and its psychology of the unconscious. Never before has
mankind been torn into two halves, and never before was the power
of absolute destruction given into the hand of man himself. It is a
"godlike" power that has fallen into human hands.

—Jung, *Letters.*

When I was barely old enough to remember, my mother took me to
the funeral parlor to view the remains of her friend Ruby Lamb. I
was excited, for the name dazzled my inner eye with wondrous images of red and white. When I looked into the casket, Ruby lay stiller
than still, with cheeks not red but white as snow and hair as soft and
pale as the fleece of a newborn lamb. The hair on my neck rose like
the hackles of a threatened dog, and I knew with perfect clarity that
something invisible lurked. If Ruby had smiled and winked at me, it
would have been no surprise. Dreadful screams ensued, and my embarrassed mother took me home.

What lived at the funeral parlor gave me a standard to apply in
other matters of the spirit. The church to which my mother took me
every week offered nothing quite so real, and I resigned from
Sunday School at the age of five. That day Miss Minish, a spinster
of 30 with liquid brown eyes and a tight mouth, had challenged her
class to imagine what we would wear to church if we were in a fron-
tier town. The other children snickered when I said I would wear
dungarees, and Miss Minish tightened her mouth still more. She
called on another little girl, who said God wanted us to wear the very
nicest clothes we had, even in the wilderness. When Miss Minish
congratulated her on knowing the right answer, I was furious. The
God I knew was not interested in the clothes I wore, and I suspected

Miss Minish of deceiving us for some dark purpose of her own.

As I grew older, my experience continued to diverge from that of the Episcopal ladies of my childhood, who seemed to believe that God shared their values. When a man I cared more about than anyone in the world died suddenly of a coronary, before he had a chance to turn fifty, grief brought me up against the inevitable question: If there were a God, or anything in the universe with more power than I, why would such a good person be allowed to die so young?

Without hope of an answer, I raged at God daily. While I raged, I painted, my hands making images beyond my conscious intent. One day I drew a picture of a clock, face up in the middle of the page. On its edge, just past 12:00, the tiny figure of a man fell backward into space. Over the scene stood a gigantic green arm with six long pointed fingers like the petals of a strange flower, perhaps a meat-eating plant. As I stared at the drawing, it came to me with crystal clarity that God does not care about the things I care about.

The idea made me angry. I thought, if God doesn't care, why should I?

Instantly the answer came back: If God doesn't care, all the more reason for you to. If you don't care, no one will.

I was stunned by the notion that my feelings counted for something in the larger scheme of things, even that the human capacity for caring might be greater than God's. Surely this was heresy.

It would be several years before I read Jung's autobiography and found comfort in the fact that he, too, was compelled to think heretical thoughts. I particularly relished the youthful vision in which he saw God's turd fall on the cathedral and shatter it. Later still I stumbled across "Answer to Job," the remarkable document in which Jung pours out his anger at the injustice and, yes, immorality of Yahweh, the Old Testament father God, coming to the shocking conclusion that Yahweh abused Job because He did not know better until Job's superior morality taught Him. That is, Jung suggests that God cannot grow except through confrontation with human values. If he is right, then my caring matters indeed.

*

One day in early spring, a new patient came to see me in my capacity as a Jungian analyst. She was caught up in an aspect of New Age thought that is not new at all, but is rooted in Victorianism's genteel respectability and a one-sided Christianity that cast evil into the unconscious two thousand years ago. This perspective promotes an illusory transcendence by encouraging repression and denial of unpleasant facts and emotions. Francie smiled all the time, but she had nightmares. She did not realize that to achieve real transcendence she would have to become conscious of the darkness in herself and in life and suffer it. Claiming an ideal childhood and a nearly perfect life now, she had no idea how bad she felt and did not want to know, but talked on and on, too fast for me to interrupt or for her to hear what she was saying.

"I keep a magic wand on my desk," she said. "When bad things happen, I wave the wand and think good thoughts."

Wondering why she thought she needed *me*, I cleared my throat to make a wedge so I could say something.

"What about evil?"

Francie was quiet for a few seconds and a shadow crossed her face, but the smile returned right away. Then she spoke in the tone of a child reciting a prayer. "I don't believe in evil. Evil is only the absence of good."

I had said enough. Probably too much. I smiled back, silently betting that she would not make a second appointment. If she did, I wondered if she would ever be able to let me in, to look at the hard dark material of her life and her dreams and talk about how she felt and the things she really cared about.

For the rest of the hour I did not interfere with the words Francie wove in the air between us, making a net to catch me if I should come too close. My eyes grew heavy and I could not focus on what she was saying. Instead, a voice in my head again asked: What about evil? And my mind went back to the thing I could not forget, the thing I had seen from the ferry the week before, on my way home through the waterways of Puget Sound.

At first I thought that what I saw on the horizon was a large black building, but we were far from land. Looking closer, I could see it moving toward us. Fast. I had been alone, standing at the rail overlooking the car deck, but now other passengers drifted out of the lounge, staring and craning their necks. An infant in its mother's arms began to cry, and an old man shouted over the wind, pointing his pipe at the thing that was going to hit us if we stayed on course. The deck was crowded by the time our engines slowed and we began to turn. Then, finally, I understood what I saw. The words leapt into my mind.

Nuclear submarine. Trident.

The baby stopped crying. In the sudden silence, the conning tower I had mistaken for a building glided past, then a shadowy body like some ancient, light-eating beast barely visible beneath the sea, blacker than any black I have ever seen. I shivered, avoiding the others' eyes. No one spoke. Hundreds of feet later the creature's fin passed, less like a shark's than the erect sting of a giant scorpion. Someone sighed, putting an end to the unnatural stillness. The baby resumed its crying. Slowly the crowd broke up, but I continued to watch the grotesque epiphany until it disappeared into the far distance.

"I would like to have seen it," said Sean, my fiancé, when I told him about it later. He had read more than I ever hoped to know about that ship. He told me it could keep going all the way around the world, and around again maybe two or three times without ever having to slow down or come to the surface. He said it carries twenty-four missiles each of which has eight or ten warheads.

"Do you know that every one of those warheads has five times the capacity of the bomb we dropped on Hiroshima?"

I did not know. I bit my lip and looked at the floor, calculating. A thousand Hiroshimas. Fifteen times the number of Jews murdered in Nazi Germany. A submerged black shadow, waiting to destroy ninety million people.

The word *evil* derives from the Indo-European root *upo*, in a variant that signifies "exceeding the proper limit." *Upo* carries the meanings "under," "up from under," and "over." The cognates of *evil* are a curiously paradoxical group of words. Some, like *up* and *above*, suggest superiority, while the prefix *sub-* and words like *valet* and *vassal* imply inferiority. *Subterfuge* carries secrecy, but *eavesdrop* and *open* reveal what is secret. Two of *evil's* relatives, *opal* and *Upanishad*, derive from a Sanskrit word that means "near to."[1] Thus, the murky origins of language hint that evil is near by, probably closer than we think. It lives in hidden corners, ready to come forth when what was closed is opened. Whenever the archetype of power is activated, whether it be power over someone or submission to another, the problem of evil lies ready to come to light. Evil is one-sided. It goes too far, now this way, now that.

It is fashionable to believe that technology has gone too far. We blame machines for the fact that human ethical consciousness may not have grown far enough to deal with the options we have created. An article typical of this perspective, published in *Whole Earth Review*, implies that computers are seductive flatterers and speed freaks, tricksters that lead writers up the garden path. Because word-processing simplifies the mechanics of writing and revision, the author suggests that computers are the demons responsible for superficial writing that bypasses the drudgery and pain of revision.

A moment's reflection reveals that people, not computers, rush through life skating over the surface of things. If they wish, people have an option that typewriters do not, to slow down and reflect upon themselves and their work. The choice is ethical, not mechanical. Laziness, superficiality, failure to reflect, haste, and susceptibility to flattery are no more qualities of machines than is bad writing. I am sometimes tempted to blame my inner devils on a mechanical companion that virtually slaps my hand, saying "bad command or file name" every time I fail to meet its inflexible requirements, but I

---

1 Except where otherwise indicated, the etymological derivations in this book are taken from William Morris, ed., *The American Heritage Dictionary of the English Language* (Boston: Houghton Mifflin, 1969). Psychological inferences drawn from the derivations are my own.

know better. Once I reclaim responsibility for myself, the machine becomes no more than a tool in the service of better work.

When I first began to reflect about these matters, I dreamed:

"I live in a house at the top of a hill on a busy city street. My car is parked on the street. When no one is looking I release the brake and give the car a little push to start it down the hill. Then I go back into the house.

"I expect to hear from the police, but half the day goes by and nothing happens. Then I get anxious and set out to discover what is going on. I walk for blocks before I finally see my car being carried away upside down like a dead animal with its paws in the air. Its top is smashed in and one side is marked by a huge starburst of fracture lines. It is obviously totaled, and I begin to realize that others may have been hurt. I wonder if anyone was killed. I imagine the police coming to the door and telling me my car got loose and ran amok and killed two people. Then I imagine walking around for the rest of my life knowing that I murdered two people. I am horribly upset. It is almost too terrible to bear."

Aside from its shadowy personal meaning for me, the dream reveals some important aspects of the relationship between technology and evil. A naive observer might conclude that my car did a terrible thing, but what happened is clearly my fault. If I stayed in the driver's seat and carried my responsibility for the vehicle, no harm would be likely to result, but looking the other way has evil consequences. I know that others may have been hurt or even killed by my unconsciousness, even though no one could prove my culpability. I can excuse myself by saying that the dream's events would never have taken place if people had not invented cars, but that is childish. Technology does exist. What has been done cannot be undone. It is time to grow up to what we have created.

A trident, says *The American Heritage Dictionary,* is "a long, three-pronged fork or weapon; especially the three-pronged spear carried by the classical god of the sea, Neptune or Poseidon."

In the language of symbolism, the sea is an image of the spiritual/psychological matrix of human life, the soup from which individual consciousness is born. Jung called this "soup" the collective unconscious. Poseidon was a bad-tempered god, the violent and unpredictable author of earthquakes and storms. Nevertheless, his enormous fertility and creative power equalled his destructiveness.

The light Christian trinity of father, son, and holy spirit is balanced by a three-pronged counterpart in the unconscious. The dark trinity consists of the qualities of the psyche that had to be repressed to permit the patriarchal development that culminated in Christianity. Satan, the unacceptable brother of Christ, is only one aspect of the dark God. Qualities of the Great Goddess comprise a second prong of the rejected trinity, while the material world of nature and the body make up a third. Thus it is that in the contemporary psyche evil, the feminine, and nature tend to be confused with one another.

Jung believed that the spiritual task of the Aquarian age would be to unite the opposites, light and dark, good and evil, requiring attitudes quite different from Francie's. He wrote,

> It will then no longer be possible to write off evil as the mere privation of good; its real existence will have to be recognized. This problem can be solved neither by philosophy, nor by economics, nor by politics, but only by the individual human being, via his experience of the living spirit.[2]

The feminist and ecology movements have already begun to differentiate two prongs of the unconscious trinity. Now we have to become conscious of the reality and locus of evil. Identifying with the good, light, true and beautiful or denying what lives in the unsavory dark have ceased to be viable options.

We the people of the United States have created Trident. Not They—not an impersonal agency of government—but We—I, my family, my friends, and all the other citizens of my country. Sean

---

2 *Aion,* CW 9ii, par. 142. [CW in the footnotes refers to *The Collected Works of C.G. Jung* (Bollingen Series XX), 20 vols., trans. R.F.C. Hull, ed. H. Read, M. Fordham, G. Adler, Wm. McGuire (Princeton: Princeton University Press, 1953-1979)]

and I calculated that every man, woman and child in the United States is responsible for 4.5 cubic inches of that ship, a total of 18,700 tons of the psyche's nuclear power, consisting of all the unacknowledged destructiveness, hatred, rage and other rejected and denied qualities of 230 million people.

What would happen if each of us took back the four and a half cubic inches that belongs to us? What would happen if we were able to be responsible for the qualities we despise in ourselves, instead of hating other people for them or projecting them on computers or Trident? What would happen if we were not afraid to care?

2
Lilith

Nothing can exist without its opposite; the two were one in the beginning and will be one again in the end. . . . Conflict engenders fire, the fire of affects and emotions, and like every other fire it has two aspects, that of combustion and that of creating light. . . . There is no change from darkness to light or from inertia to movement without emotion.

—Jung, "Psychological Aspects of the Mother Archetype."

Sean and I had an argument. I went to a restaurant and ate alone, pretending to myself that I did not care. In my dream that night:

"I go out alone to eat. As I walk into the restaurant I get entangled with a young couple and their child. The little boy is in some kind of trouble and I help him. My intervention creates a sense of mutual obligation between the couple and me, because of which we wind up sitting together. I ask the woman her name. She ignores me. I persist. After I repeat the question several times she finally tells me her name. It is Lilith."

Lilith was the original feminist. According to Jewish legend she was made of the same earth as Adam and became his first wife, long before God created Eve from Adam's rib.[3] Lilith was beautiful and seductive, with long flowing hair and the wings of an angel, but she was smart, too. She and Adam quarreled because he wanted to dominate her. She refused to submit to him, pointing out that they were equal because they were made of the same substance. When Adam insisted that she had to obey him, she swore and flew away.

Adam complained to Yahweh, who agreed that Lilith was wrong and sent three angels to bring her back. She was enraged. The angels

---

[3] Nathan Ausubel, *A Treasury of Jewish Folklore* (New York: Crown Publishers, 1948), pp. 593-594.

threatened to drown her in the Red Sea, but Lilith would not yield and they had to let her go. She has flown at the head of hosts of evil spirits ever since, a storm goddess and demon of the night who lurks in isolated places, howling her hatred in the voice of an owl. A dangerous temptress of men, she is also reputed to kill helpless infants to avenge the wrongs done to her millenia ago. Mothers have to protect their newborn children with amulets inscribed with the three angels' names and the words "Lilith be gone." Boy babies are safe from her after a week of life, but girls are vulnerable for twenty days.

Although it was not a complete surprise, I was not exactly pleased to find a she-demon of Lilith's stature living in my psyche. Still, Lilith began life as a decent enough sort, an independent woman who only wanted equal status with her husband, exactly the kind of relationship I wanted with Sean. She did not get mean until the male power interests ganged up on her. I could not blame her for refusing to give in to them. If Sean and a patriarchal God and three male angels kept trying to tell me how wrong I was, I would have done the same. I *have* done the same.

The more I thought about it, the clearer it became that the archetype of Lilith must be buried in every psyche in the Judeo-Christian world, men and women alike, filling us with horror and shame at the rage and vengefulness we harbor in the depths. Because the independent feminine spirit was rejected at the very beginning of the Judeo-Christian development, it turned perverse. The repressed Lilith in each of us takes revenge by killing children; that is, by attacking whatever is young and undeveloped in ourselves and others. Having been abused, she becomes an abuser, embodying the mean thing inside that kicks a cat or speaks harshly to a child because small animals and children cannot fight back. With sarcastic remarks, she cuts down fragile new life before it can grow strong enough to survive the force of her contempt. She is manipulative, and misuses sex to give her power. If you cannot express love because you feel too vulnerable, if you are afraid to care lest you become dependent, look for Lilith.

*

Summer had come. It was time to split the firewood that would heat my house the following winter. As I worked, I mused about my dream. Lilith must need something from me, I thought, for gods and demons are not ordinarily willing to divulge their names. If you know someone's true name, it gives you power over them. Considering her fear of vulnerability, it was a small miracle that Lilith had revealed herself to me.

While I split wood in the outside world, my mind becomes engaged in active imagination, a procedure for relating to relatively inaccessible parts of the psyche.[4] I imagine going to the restaurant where Lilith and I first met, and find her where she was in the dream, her chin resting on the palm of one hand while the fingers of the other drum on the table near an open pack of cigarettes. Her plate has been pushed aside and the ashtray holds three crushed butts. Her husband is quietly finishing his meal. He is wearing a startling red corduroy shirt with brown corduroy pants like the ones Sean wears. Their son is the most beautiful toddler I have ever seen, with a shock of black hair like his father's, contrasting with the bright blue eyes and pale red-head's skin inherited from his mother. He is solemnly spooning up his food.

I sit down next to Lilith and ask her to tell me her husband's name. She reaches for a cigarette and rolls her eyes toward the ceiling. With an air of elaborately calculated patience she growls, "Adam, asshole."

I wince. "I'll appreciate it if you won't call me names. Especially that one. It's repulsive."

"Yes, isn't it," she says with a satisfied smile. "All the old words are so overused they have lost their power. 'Asshole,' now . . . it's still good."

"If you misuse it, it'll lose its power too. You've wasted it on me. How would *I* know the man you're with is Adam? You divorced him

---

[4] See my chapter, "Active Imagination in Practice," in Murray Stein, ed., *Jungian Analysis* (La Salle, Illinois: Open Court, 1982), pp. 173-191.

way back at the beginning of time."

"We decided to have another go at it. That wimp Eve didn't work out like he thought she was going to. A few millenia of living with nothing but niceness almost put him to sleep forever. He finally realized he needs me to keep him growing. Right, Adam?"

Adam looks up long enough to flash a lively smile, but says nothing. I turn back to Lilith, and approach another topic. "What are you doing here, anyway? I never asked for you. I just came here to have a little dinner and bam . . . ! Here you are, all mixed up in my life."

"I've been in your family for generations. On your father's side. There was Gracie Mae, for instance . . ."

Returning abruptly to the everyday world, I shuddered and took a whack at a billet of wood with my splitting maul. Good Night! Was that bitch implying that I have anything in common with *Gracie Mae?* I scanned the wood I had cut for pairs of equal-sized pieces to start a nice even stack.

Gracie Mae was the grandmother who used to pinch my bottom and call me "Babe." I was not the only one who hated her. On holidays, when she came to dinner, my father always got a migraine and disappeared. Sometimes he disappeared *before* she got there. Later the sound of his retching in the bathroom would filter through the dinner-table conversation that would get to politics and religion sooner or later. Then Grandad always pounded the table and waved his cigar around, and my mother would try to change the subject while Gracie Mae egged everyone on. My father would not be seen for the rest of the day.

After Grandad died, my mother sacrificed me to Gracie Mae. Once a month I had to go with her to have lunch at the Hotel. Finally one day I dug in my heels and refused. I imagine I have Lilith to thank for saying no.

When I start to work on the next batch of wood, the restaurant comes into focus again. "Go on," I say to Lilith. "Tell me where else in my past you appeared."

"If you have to know, your Aunt Betty was the last one I could get into until you came along."

That makes me feel better. Aunt Betty, my father's sister, left home long before I was born, and went to New York where she and her husband Ray got into radio. Uncle Ray was Raymond on Inner Sanctum. When I was small we went to New York and saw the squeaky door that was really only half a door they used for Inner Sanctum's sound effects. Uncle Ray said somebody new at the station oiled the door once, and when air time came they were all in deep shit.

Aunt Betty was pretty and had long red hair. I can still hear my mother's scandalized voice talking about the time Betty came home for a visit when she was FORTY and went for a walk with her hair down to her WAIST, with no shoes on in PUBLIC. Whew! My mother's hot breath almost curled my hair, and I did not dare ask what was wrong with having your hair down in public. I thought it was pretty.

After Betty split up with Ray, the ladies of the Episcopal Church talked about her in hushed tones. Once I overheard the words DI-VORCED WOMAN. Someone said she even SLEPT WITH MEN, whatever that meant.

Lilith had come a long way from Gracie Mae by the time she got into Aunt Betty.

"Thank God for Aunt Betty," I say to her. "Just knowing she was walking through Manhattan in her long hair and SLEEPING WITH MEN kept me from suffocating in our mutual home town. It must have been miserable for her to be the kind of person she was in the world of her generation."

When I thought about that, it put a different light on my grand-mother. Gracie Mae was a Victorian. For someone of her generation to be dominated by Lilith's spirit must have been a fate worse than death. No wonder she was a bitch on wheels, just like Lilith when the angels tried to drown her. I felt lucky that Grandma had not found an opportunity to drop me on my head during my first twenty days of life.

Turning to Lilith I say, "I wish I had told Aunt Betty how important she was to me before she died. Trouble is, I didn't really know it until a few years ago. If it was you who gave her her spirit, you can't be all bad."

Lilith sits up straight and crushes her cigarette in the ashtray. The atmosphere has turned frigid. Wondering if she is going to hit me, I push my chair back from the table. The look she sends my way makes me shrivel. She speaks in a cold, hard voice. "What do you mean, bad?"

"Don't you know what kind of a reputation you have? Where I come from, it's terrible."

"Where you come from STINKS."

I do not know what to do. Lilith's face is pinched and miserable. When I put out my hand to touch her she jerks away, drawing herself up like the insulted caterpillar in *Alice in Wonderland*. I see that anything I do will be wrong and sit still, hardly breathing.

When she speaks her voice is flat, betraying the hopelessness I hear over and over again from women who consult me about depression. "You wouldn't smell so great either if you'd been tramped on for six fucking millenia."

"Has it been that long? God! No wonder you're enraged."

"Damned right I'm mad. Assholes keep spitting on me. Think they can get away with it because I'm a woman. I'll show 'em."

"Look, I understand all too well how you feel. You have a lot of good reasons for it. Centuries and centuries of reasons. But I have to tell you something. It's not right to take it out on that beautiful child. Please stop being mean to him."

Lilith gives the boy a quick, sour look, then stares down at the table, silently biting her lip. I say, "Well? How about it?"

She shrugs. "I don't know what to say. It gets away from me. The fuckers make me so mad I wind up hitting the kid."

"Well, if you don't stop it, you and Adam will create a world exactly like the one he made with Eve, and the next six thousand years will be no different from the last. Or worse. If you don't mend your ways, we'll blow up the planet before that boy has a chance to grow up."

Just then the child gives me a radiant smile. The thought that he might not live out his life is almost more than I can bear. He is an old soul, with a clear, gentle, patient look far beyond his years. Although I suspect that Lilith has abused him badly, he is either unaffected by it or has already achieved the wisdom that suffering can confer. Feeling tearful, I turn to Lilith and ask the boy's name.

Her eyes narrow. Pushing her chair back from the table, she blows three perfect smoke rings and watches them rise. I wait. Finally she says, "His name is Li. Spelled L I, not L E E."

Was the name taken from the first two syllables of *Lilith?* It sounded Oriental. Could there be something in Eastern thought that would help resolve the psychological, spiritual, and social problems that Lilith's exile has created?

It was time for a break from the woodpile. I went into my house and sat down with a cup of tea and my copy of the *I Ching,* the Chinese book sometimes used to bring ancient Eastern wisdom to bear on current problems. Each of the book's sixty-four hexagrams resembles a meditation on an elemental natural pattern. The one called "Li" has the subtitle "The Clinging, Fire." It says:

> Fire has no definite form but clings to the burning object and thus is bright. As water pours down from heaven, so fire flames up from the earth. . . . Li stands for nature in its radiance.
>
> THE JUDGMENT
> The Clinging. Perseverance furthers.
> It brings success.
> Care of the cow brings good fortune.

> What is dark clings to what is light and so enhances the brightness of the latter. A luminous thing giving out light must have within itself something that perseveres; otherwise it will in time burn itself out. Everything that gives light is dependent on something to which it clings, in order that it may continue to shine.
>
> Thus sun and moon cling to heaven, and grain, grass, and trees cling to the earth. So, too, the twofold clarity of the dedicated man clings to what is right and thereby can shape the world. Human life on earth is conditioned and unfree, and when man recognizes this limitation and makes himself dependent upon the harmonious and

beneficent forces of the cosmos, he achieves success. The cow is the symbol of extreme docility. By cultivating in himself an attitude of compliance and voluntary dependence, man acquires clarity without sharpness and finds his place in the world.[5]

I considered how Lilith's wish for independent and equal status with the masculine makes her afraid of the dependency that belongs to the child in us all. How natural it is for her to protect herself from hurt and rejection by trying to be invulnerable. What a paradox that she, like all archetypes, must rely on people to give her life in the human world, just as fire depends on the wood it burns. The dependence is mutual, however, for without the divine fire our lives are devoid of warmth and light, passion and meaning. Of what use is firewood unless it is burned?

For the first time I could see the roots of my personal urge for autonomy in ancient energy called by the name of Lilith. I had long been troubled by something that happened whenever I felt the weight of dependency, mine on others or theirs on me. All too often I would explode with rage that I myself could not comprehend. Now I saw the source of the anger. The Lilith in me chafed at the constraining bonds of relationship. If I could accept *her* deeply enough, perhaps she could accept *my* human needs and allow the childlike, dependent parts of me to live.

Back at the restaurant I say, "Listen, Lilith. It's terribly difficult to live with you. You push me so hard and fill me with such rage when you're frustrated that I feel like a volcano sometimes. In the outside world, people react so strongly to you—the good parts of you as well as the bad—that I can hardly stand it. You make my life utterly impossible. But at the same time . . . I have to tell you that you also make my life worth living."

Suddenly her hard, cynical exterior drops away. She looks me straight in the eye. "I'm grateful to you for bearing me," she says.

---

[5] *The I Ching or Book of Changes,* trans. Richard Wilhelm and Cary F. Baynes, 3rd ed. (Princeton: Princeton University Press, 1967), pp. 118-119.

"Please don't give up."

I am amazed at the change in her, and suddenly feel tearful. "I don't want to give up. But *please* try to understand my need to live a human life. Please don't mistreat that beautiful child any more."

Lilith silently gives me her hand.

I placed a billet on the chopping block, raised the splitting maul and focused on an unseen spot deep in the center of the wood. When the maul came down, the wood fell into two neat halves. I caught my breath and began a new stack with the matching pieces. Then I picked up another billet.

Dependence and autonomy, love of others and love of self: these are the halves of woman. The part of a woman that is like Eve puts her man first. She is, above all, Adam's rib. Eve wants nothing so much as to make a man happy by living up to his ideal image of woman. Lilith requires something different. The part of a woman that is like her is independent, creative, and unable to conform to patriarchal cultural patterns. The emergence of Lilith into a woman's conscious life often marks the beginning of her individual development. Only then can she stop unconsciously going along with things and begin to think for herself.

Because Lilith can make relationships with men difficult, a woman may try to repress her Lilith side. Then it comes out in rage and vengefulness, overt or hidden. Hidden, it sometimes becomes a perverse kind of not-caring, a denial of feeling that is grounded in Lilith's fear of dependency. Thus, a woman who is afraid to risk being dependent may hurt others and violate her own feelings by pretending that the people and things she loves the most are not important.

In the most primal depths of the psyche, Eve and Lilith carry the two halves of feminine wholeness. For several millenia, Eve dominated Western culture. Lilith has scarcely been permitted to exist. In recent years, however, the feminist movement has brought this figure into the light, where her positive qualities have a chance to overcome the negativity that results from repression.

Lilith lives in the psyches of men as well as women. She may push a man beyond the traditional Adam-Eve type of marriage into a man-woman relationship in which dominance is not the issue. A man whose feminine aspect has a strong Lilith component tends to be attracted to the Lilith in a woman. A Lilith type of woman will not make him comfortable, as the Eve type would. However, if he can bear Lilith's fire she has the power to transform him, for Lilith serves the development of a man's individuality, not conventionally stereotyped masculine attitudes.

The appearance of Lilith-like qualities in women in recent films and books is a measure of the toehold this demon-goddess has gained in contemporary life, perhaps on her way to cultural acceptance and integration. For example, *Trial by Wilderness,* a young-adult novel by David Mathieson,[6] portrays Lilith's spirit at its best as it emerges in the book's heroine.

Seventeen-year-old Elena Bradbury is a bright and self-reflective young Canadian woman, raised by her father and the "thou shalt nots" of her dour Aunt Agatha. She has planned to follow in her father's footsteps as a scientist, but the small plane in which she is traveling crashes en route to her father's expedition. When her heroic efforts to save the plane's pilot are unsuccessful, Elly is left alone in an isolated corner of British Columbia's coastal forest. Thus, at the very outset, this youngster's patriarchal path is blocked and she is thrust back to live or die in the realm of the Great Mother. Unlike the original Garden of Eden, however, this garden has neither an Adam nor a father God. Elly's survival depends on her capacity to touch a feminine spirit as tough and independent as Lilith's, for Eve's docile and conciliatory nature will not serve her in the uninhabited wilderness.

The young woman confronts the dark powers in herself and in nature with extraordinary courage and resourcefulness, and as she struggles to save her physical life, she works out her spiri-

---

[6] Boston: Houghton Mifflin, 1985.

tual/psychological salvation. The only available help is within her. She takes full advantage of her rich inner life, manifest in dreams, self-reflection, and imaginary conversations with her sturdy friend Pauline. Tempted to start a conflagration that would almost certainly attract rescuers, she makes the ethical choice not to save herself at the expense of the wilderness and its creatures. Later, when she realizes that her father has encouraged her to sacrifice her own nature to his wishes, fiery anger flares and she resolves, Lilith-like, that she will no longer subordinate herself to him. Her rage softens when she understands that pain over the death of his beautiful young wife is what compelled her father to cling to her. Then she can forgive him, calling upon the same ethical compassion to moderate the fire of Lilith's wrath with which she earlier contained the demonic urge to start a literal forest fire.

By the time she makes her way back to civilization, Elly has become an independent individual. As Mathieson puts it, "She had earned her status the hard way, and the time of passivity, of *going along* with whatever others might plan was over. Her father was a determined man, but now she knew a thing or two herself about determination!"

With the first autumn storm, Elly realizes that she must wait no longer. She sets out in *Water Bird*, the one-woman vessel she has laboriously built, embodying her reborn spirit. She finds that she *cannot* go north toward the island where her father is camped. The change in her will not permit it. Henceforth Elly will live her own life.

Her determination has yet to be tested, however. By the time a passing ocean liner picks her up, she has run out of drinking water and is nearing the end of her physical resources. When she asks the ship's captain to bring her small vessel aboard along with her, he is contemptuous and abusive, authoritarian to the point of madness. In a startling denouement, Elly flies off like Lilith, taking from the rescuing ship only the soda pop she needs to keep her from dying of thirst. She is last seen in *Water Bird*, paddling for the mainland. Elena Bradbury's hard-won individuality is too precious to give up for the safety of patriarchal attitudes that have gone too far.

The question now is this: Can we bear Lilith's emergence? Will those whose fate is to help restore this fiery demon-goddess to her rightful place in the human psyche be adequate vessels for the process? If the reconciling child of the future is to live, we will have to take a lesson from Elly Bradbury and let Lilith's wrath burn through first to autonomy, then to human compassion and forgiveness.

There is much to forgive.

3
Falling

I suffered and was miserable, but it seems that life was never wanting and in the blackest night even, and just there, by the grace of God, I could see a Great Light. Somewhere there seems to be a great kindness in the abysmal darkness of the deity.

—Jung, Letter in *Psychological Perspectives.*

In a manner of speaking, Francie and the blue pelican fell together.

Soon after Sean and I were married, a package arrived in the mail with the return address of a former lover. Jake, an artist, had offered me a wedding gift of a ceramic sculpture he had created during our years together. I remembered the piece with affection and looked forward to renewing my acquaintance with the fanciful blue pelican nesting among extra-terrestrial reeds, made with the charm and grace that typified Jake's work.

My heart sank when I opened the box. Wrapped only in a few pages of crumpled newspaper, the pelican lay in shards. My stomach churned and I wanted to cry. Did Jake not value his work enough to protect it, I wondered, or was he unconsciously telling me something? Had the news of my marriage shattered him like the sculpture? Or was something entirely different going on, something I knew nothing about? I replaced the lid, unable to face the myriad possibilities or decide what to do with the poor wounded creature. Sean could mend almost anything, but this, I thought, would be beyond him. Some of the pieces were tiny, many no more than dust.

After we finished dinner that night, I brought the box to the kitchen table where we were sitting. Sean stared at the fragments as if communing with them. He picked up the bird's intact head and fitted it to a segment of neck. Musing, he tried a piece here, another there.

"It's like a jigsaw puzzle," he said.

Carefully he put the shards in a bucket. In the morning, he got out the superglue and set to work.

Meanwhile Francie, the blissed-out New Age patient who had begun analysis the previous spring, had taken to the work far better than I had dared to hope. Slowly she found the courage to face her nightmare pursuers, and the counterfeit smile dropped from her face. The first week in December, a few days after the pelican came, she limped into my office on crutches.

"I couldn't believe it," she said. "I was walking down the street, overflowing with Christmas spirit, when all of a sudden I was flat on my face on the asphalt. The last thing I thought before I hit was, 'Oh God no! I'm going to break my glasses,' just like when I was a little kid. My parents were so poor it was a disaster when I broke my glasses. I did it over and over again. I couldn't help it. After it happened a few times, I felt worse about the money for the glasses than the endless skinned knees and sprained ankles. And those awful brown high-top oxfords my mother made me wear to support my weak ankles . . ."

She thrust out her foot, revealing a pair of fashionable new high-top walking shoes. "Can you believe I have to wear them again?"

"Wait a minute," I said. "You told me nothing bad ever happened when you were a child."

She winced. "Well . . . I forgot some things. I forgot about falling down, and . . ." She sighed and made a rueful face. "I forgot a lot."

"What was going on before you fell?" I asked.

"When I was little?"

"No . . . last week."

Francie stared at me through her half-inch thick spectacles, and I stared back through mine. "Nothing. Well . . . my brother left a message on my phone machine that he wasn't coming for Christmas. I was upset at first. I wanted to make a nice Christmas for him now that he's alone. I'd made a lot of plans. . . . Then I thought, never mind. The plans can be changed. It's no skin off my nose if Charles doesn't want to come. It's fine. Wonderful. He's so hard to be with since his wife died, I'd rather not spend Christmas with him any-

way. Actually, he's *always* been hard to be with. I'm only just be-ginning to notice."

She was silent. Then she laughed. "After I got the phone mes-sage, I went for a walk and fell on my face. Maybe I felt worse than I thought. Maybe I felt rotten."

After our first, inauspicious meeting, it had occurred to me that I might have underestimated Francie. Perhaps the reason I disliked her, I thought, was because she resembled a part of myself that I wanted to disown. The hidden Janet was so different from the way I thought of myself that I could hardly believe she was there, but when I was tired or under stress, out she would come. Then I would act falsely cheerful and try to deny my feelings, especially the painful ones, just like Francie. I would honestly believe that I did not care about some painful thing that had happened, but then an accident or an unexpected argument with the person who had hurt my feelings would force me to see that underneath I felt wounded or angry or afraid. In case I should miss the point, Francie and I were the same age and resembled each other physically.

Until I faced certain things about myself, Francie set my teeth on edge and my covert dislike affected her in hidden ways. Once I re-claimed the Janet in the shadows, however, I began to like Francie and could wait patiently for insight to come in its own way and its own time. After all, I was still making new discoveries about myself every day, after thirty years of work with my unconscious. I could hardly expect a patient to know herself deeply in nine short months.

Francie's early memories were few and far between. As a result, talk about her childhood had an abstract, airy quality. She said she had grown up in a beautiful natural setting, a kind of Garden of Eden where it was safe to run wild and free. She told me she was sure her basic needs had been met. Then she had a dream:

"I am a teacher, and it is time to give my early-elementary pupils their first-quarter examination. The examination will be at 1:00. I have waited until that morning to make up the questions, and am searching through the textbook for appropriate material. There is hardly any content in this part of the book. I have to pull the questions out of nothing, almost out of the air."

Francie's weekly meetings with me were at 1:00. Her failure to find subject-matter upon which to examine the dream children was like her inability to remember much about the first quarter of her fifty years. But a few days after the dream, sudden pain from a sprained ankle and scraped knee and the image of her hand thrust out to catch herself, glasses falling headlong to the pavement, reminded her forcibly of painful childhood experiences, thrusting her abruptly out of Paradise into hard reality.

True to the promise of the Old-Testament serpent, Francie's eyes were opened and she became like God, knowing not only good but also evil.[7] Unpleasant fragments of memory surfaced, along with a welter of disagreeable emotions: rage, anguish, anxiety, depression. To deal with the flood of material, I suggested that we work together daily for the three weeks until Christmas.

Slowly, carefully, she put her puzzle together. Many pieces were missing, but she filled in gaps in her memory with snapshots and family stories. She showed me pictures of a thin, shy-looking little girl with dark wispy pigtails and a tucked-in chin. Her look and manner were startlingly like those of a child I had evaluated for abuse the year before, a little girl who cowered and cried out when I raised my hand to turn on the light.

Francie's story was not dramatic, however. As far as she could recall, there was no overt violence or blatant sexual abuse. The picture that emerged revealed nothing worse than neglect, deprivation, and small, veiled cruelties.

She remembered sitting under a meager Christmas tree, caressing the packages that bore her name, yearning to feel the shape of a book beneath the wrappings. One Christmas Eve before she turned five, she lay awake the whole night, listening for sleigh bells and praying for a book from Santa Claus. More than forty years later, she still had bright, sharp images of a dozen or so books from the Christmases and birthdays of her childhood. Lovingly she recalled their

---

[7] See Genesis 3.

names and described the forms and colors of pristine dust jackets.

"Francie," I asked, "Didn't you have any toys?"

She closed her eyes and wrinkled her forehead. "Well, yes," she finally acknowledged. "There were my brother's things. After he went to college I had his toys."

"When was that?"

"When I was five, I think. Maybe six."

She described a wagon, battered and rusty, the broken pieces of an electric train, and an abandoned chemistry set. Although she never had a bicycle of her own, when she was ten she had assembled one from the dismembered parts she found in the garage.

I pressed her. "Wasn't there something that was *yours?* A doll? A stuffed animal?"

A look of pain crossed her face. "I had a teddy bear when I was a baby," she said. "He and I were quarantined when I was two and had a contagious disease. When I got well they burned the bear. I loved him."

"And when you were older? Wasn't there anything to play with besides your brother's toys?"

"This is too hard," she said. "I don't want to talk about it any more today." I could understand how she felt. I was drained. The hour was not over, but I was glad to let her go.

The next day she told me about losing her miniature collection. Hoarding the dimes that were her weekly allowance, she had bought tiny animals and people, tools, vehicles, furniture, trees . . . a whole world of diminutive things. The day she took the miniatures to school and showed them to her third-grade classmates, her locker was ransacked, most of her treasures stolen or broken. The teacher did not believe her, and Francie had no way to recover the tiny world she had so lovingly created.

"That was when I began to give up," she told me. "Even now I feel hopeless when I remember that no one would help me get my miniatures back. The most precious thing I had, the only thing that was mine, was gone."

My mind kept going back to the packages under the tree. There must have been *something* in them. "Francie, what did you get for Christmas besides books?"

She laughed. It was not a nice laugh. "Underwear. Mittens. A sweater, if I was lucky. The thing I could count on was mittens."

She described fat, brightly-colored wool yarn from which her mother knit mittens. Only little kids had their mittens attached to strings, but even after she turned ten, Francie threaded a string for her mittens through the arms of her coat every Christmas afternoon. The words of a long-forgotten poem came back to her, and she recited in a sing-song voice: "Three little kittens lost their mittens and they began to cry. Meow, meow, meow."

Francie's father had lost his money in the Depression, and she knew without being told that each pair of mittens had to last through the long Minnesota winter and on until the next December 25. After the Depression, there was no money because her brother was in college on the west coast.

Francie's mother had aspirations for Charles, the firstborn son and the only boy child to survive infancy. When Cal Tech accepted him before he turned sixteen, his renown in Francie's home town was no greater than she or her mother knew he deserved. His advent every Christmas vacation was of vastly more significance to Francie than the Christ child's. She longed for his attention with at least as much intensity as she hoped for a book.

Now Francie's remembering converged upon Charles. She recalled waking in the night and calling for her mother. She was frantic and desperate when Charles came instead, but he refused to get her mother. For the first time she understood that he had been her primary caretaker for several years. Her parents, who had little interest in raising a daughter so late in their lives, had given her to her brother as if she were an intelligent and expensive toy. She fascinated Charles and, for better or worse, he was there for her whenever he was not in school. He alone relieved her isolation and stood between her and their unhappy parents, who were locked together in poisonous mutual hatred.

Shortly after Francie's sixth birthday, the one who had been omnipresent disappeared. She did not recall Charles' leaving, but what she knew of the ensuing years was barren indeed, as if the sun had gone out and abandoned her to a permanently gray landscape. That was when the falling began. It happened so often that her knees were rarely free of scabs or fresh wounds. As she remembered it, she was sick almost as much as not, and perpetually alone except for the vacation times when Charles came home.

According to the mythology of their family, which both of them believed implicitly, Charles and Francie adored each other. However, her actual memories were uniformly painful and contrasted sharply with the fantasy. The brother and sister were virtually inseparable all right, but it was not love that united them. Charles looked to the little girl to fill his emptiness while she waited in vain for him to validate her.

Soon after we began to talk about these matters, Francie dreamed:

"I have an appointment to have my urine analyzed. When I urinate into a test tube, it immediately fills with a white precipitate. I am startled. I take the tube to the doctor's to find out what it means. The waiting room is crowded, even though it is early morning. I try to get to the desk to leave the urine sample. Others get in the way and it is almost noon before I can turn my sample over to the nurse. My intention is to go home now, but the nurse, in a voice fraught with significance, says that smart people wait for their test results. I decide I'd better wait. More time passes and I am still waiting."

I mused. "Do you know what *precipitate* means?"

"You know," said Francie. "Like snow. White stuff separating out of a solution."

"I mean the root of the word. Its deeper meaning."

We looked it up. The Latin root *praecipitare* means "to throw headlong." One of *precipitate's* definitions is "To fall headlong," just as Francie had fallen. The dream hints that Francie's fall was not entirely "black" or destructive. To view the painful event as a diagnostic tool in the service of self-understanding would permit its "white," light-giving aspect to become visible.

In the dream, trying to be smart kept Francie suspended, waiting for a doctor who never materialized. In outer reality, intellectual achievement was her family's highest value. Charles won approval for his good grades in school, and when he left home, Francie followed in his footsteps, compensating for the nurturance she lacked by being "the smart one." However, when she was eight, Charles tried unsuccessfully to teach her calculus, all the while believing that only perversity kept the bright little girl from learning the strange symbols he thrust at her. As she waited in vain for the doctor in the dream, so she waited for Charles to affirm that she was smart enough to suit him.

It seemed to Francie that she spent her whole childhood waiting for Charles. Each time he returned to college she would promptly begin to wait for his next visit, like a puppet waiting for the one who knew how to pull her strings. When he was not there, she felt empty. When he came home, hope for his approval filled her. She waited for him as for a savior. But *what* a savior, a god as arbitrary and unpredictable as Yahweh.

The third time I read "Answer to Job," in which Jung rages against Yahweh's injustice, ruthlessness, and emotional unreliability, I was struck by the resemblance between the Old Testament God and a narcissistic father, a role that in Francie's case was played by her brother. As Alice Miller has documented so well,[8] such a parent or parent substitute does not value his children for who they are because he sees them as extensions of himself. Similarly, Jung says of Yahweh:

> The character thus revealed fits a personality who can only convince himself that he exists through his relation to an object. Such dependence on the object is absolute when the subject is totally lacking in self-reflection and therefore has no insight into himself. It is as if he existed only by reason of the fact that he has an object which assures him that he is really there.[9]

Perhaps Yahweh, a god who can only be conscious of himself

---

[8] *The Drama of the Gifted Child* (New York: Basic Books, 1981).
[9] "Answer to Job," *Psychology and Religion,* CW 11, par. 574.

through the suffering of his children, is the archetype in whose image the narcissistic father is made. Children who have a certain inner strength can be pushed to a pinnacle of moral development by the unconscious cruelty of such a parent. In that case, abuse becomes "part of that power which would ever work evil but engenders good."[10] But not all children have the capacity to grow through suffering. For those who do not, narcissistic parenting can destroy the possibility that they will ever function as mature and independent adults.

My colleague Erika, who studied families of psychotic children, told me that the dominant parent in such families often unconsciously communicates three things to his children: 1) the parent has superior knowledge, ability, and expertise in all matters, and it must never be challenged; 2) dire consequences will ensue if the child engages in independent or creative activity not sanctioned by the parent; and 3) the child is weak, defective, or otherwise inferior, but is nonetheless deeply loved by the all-powerful parent.

"A child reared in this kind of family," said Erika, "has an excellent chance of never growing up at all." She herself had been raised in Nazi Germany and said the Third Reich resembled the dysfunctional families in her research. In Hitler's relationship with "his people" she saw the deadly triad of communications described above. As if to underscore the point, she committed suicide, terminating a lifelong struggle to come to terms with the collective insanity of her childhood.

I learned from Francie that a sibling's effect on a child can be as decisive as that of a parent. In her life, Charles was the superior one who appeared to love her in spite of the overwhelming evidence he provided that she was inadequate. It made her uncomfortable to see it, but he was like a sadistic lover who unconsciously suspended her in a perpetual state of unrequited love.

"There's this memory I keep pushing away," she said, but it

---

10 Philip Wayne, trans., *Goethe, Faust* (Baltimore: Penguin, 1949), part 1, act 1.

won't leave me alone. It's embarrassing. It has a strange feeling about it, almost like a dream, but I'm pretty sure it really happened."

One day when she was sitting on the toilet, Charles came naked into the bathroom. He must have been nineteen or twenty, she thought, and she ten or eleven. She saw then what she had never seen before, the thing hanging between his legs. She had seen her father's penis many times, red and shriveled like the head of the Thanksgiving turkey her mother got from a farmer each year. This was something different, a pale and swollen thing that excited an unfamiliar sensation in the pit of her stomach. Charles did not look at Francie, but gazed at his face in the mirror for a long long time, as if she were not there. Francie felt the air throb with unseen life. She was fascinated, but also afraid. Charles glanced at her with an enigmatic smile and left the room without speaking. Her face burned. She did not know why, but she could never again look Charles in the eye.

"Do you suppose he remembers that?" I asked.

Francie shook her head. "I doubt it. He hardly noticed I was there. Anyway, I'm certainly not going to ask." She blushed.

I imagine she was right. Different members of a family rarely remember the same events. It is not that our memories deceive us, but they highlight what is relevant to our individual psyches. When my own brother and I talked about our mother, I was shocked to learn that the person I remembered bore no resemblance to the one he described. "We must have had different mothers!" I said, and for all practical purposes it was so, for we had not come into her life at the same time and she treated us differently.

Certain patterns in Francie's relationship with Charles were etched so deeply on her psyche that they recurred repeatedly with the men she loved in her adult life. She would put herself entirely in a man's hands at first, trying to please him as she had wanted to please Charles. Unconsciously, however, she was sure her lover would abandon her, as Charles had, and would watch him like a hawk. At the first sign that she had displeased him, she would turn against him, telling him in various ways, "I don't care. I don't need you." If she persisted, the man would sooner or later fulfill her expectation and leave.

At times she suffered something akin to the flashbacks of war veterans with post-traumatic stress syndrome. A whiff of condescension on a lover's face, a cold or sarcastic edge to his voice, could plunge her into an intolerable admixture of rage and shame over which she had no control. It was as if she stepped into a hole in her psyche and fell straight down to childhood emotions that she did not remember directly, but repeatedly reexperienced. In Jungian language, she fell into a complex.

As Francie and I talked about these patterns, she became enraged at her brother. Months later she would realize that he, a child of eleven when she was born, was as much a victim of circumstance as she. Then she could say, "He must have been as desperate as I was. I had *him* for a few years at least, but he didn't have anyone until he was eleven, and then he got a baby to take care of. Poor guy."

Now, however, anger came up like the bubbles in a boiling pot, and with anger came more memories.

In the November of her tenth year, Francie came down with a cold and stayed home from school, dozing on the davenport and listening to the radio. Her favorite soap opera was interrupted by a news report about a fire at a famous Los Angeles night spot. Calling it a holocaust, the announcer said that hundreds of people had been killed. When her father came home for lunch, Francie pretended to be asleep. She heard her mother say, "Dan, there was a terrible fire."

"I already know about it," he said.

Her mother's voice trembled. "I'm so worried about Charles. Couldn't we call him?"

Listening, Francie was shocked. Her parents hardly ever made long-distance telephone calls, and when they did, it was on Sunday when the rates were low.

"I tried to call him," said her father. "He wasn't in." There was a pause. As soon as her mother began to cry her father went on. "An unidentified Cal Tech man died in the fire."

Behind the tragic note in his voice, Francie detected something else, something resembling satisfaction. She knew her father never let an opportunity pass to twist a knife in her mother's heart, but this time it twisted in her heart too. She went rigid with anguish. She did not believe she could go on living if Charles were dead. Waves washed over her, waves from a sea she had never seen in the outside world. She thought she was going to throw up. Then there was nothing.

When she regained consciousness, her parents were finishing their lunch. Francie went to the bathroom and examined her face in the mirror. Perhaps it was a little pale, she thought, but otherwise she looked the same as she always did. She went back to the davenport and slept until the next day.

I recoiled. It was all too easy to imagine how she had felt. "My God, Francie. Didn't you ask your parents about it?"

"It didn't occur to me. They never talked to me about anything real. It seems like I was born knowing they couldn't or wouldn't help me with things that mattered. I didn't even think they *should* help. It wasn't what parents *did.*" Her forehead wrinkled. "I don't get it. I've always thought they were really good parents."

"It was all you knew," I said. "Until you get outside what you were born into, there's no way to see it. You just assume it's the same for everyone. I imagine your parents were doing the best they could, but you were terribly isolated and deprived. It must have been awful for you."

Unexpectedly, Francie began to sob. I had never seen her cry before. Now, for the first time, she could feel the pain of the lonely little girl she had been.

When she could speak again, she resumed her story. For weeks she did not know whether Charles was alive or dead. To spare herself a pain too great for her young psyche to bear, she simply separated herself from her attachment to him. For forty years those feelings remained childish and unaltered, in a dark corner of her psyche, but to her conscious mind they ceased to exist. By the time Charles came home for Christmas that year, he no longer mattered.

Although she could not be certain, Francie believed it was then that the savior first came to her. She was able to sacrifice her need for Charles because someone else was available, a redeemer who came to heal her wounds and fill the emptiness of her days as Charles never could. She remembered lying in bed for hours, imagining a scene of an intensity and color that contrasted sharply with the somber cast of her outer life. If her mother interrupted her fantasy she would reply, "I'll be there pretty soon. I'm thinking."

He was not at all like your average savior. He bore no resemblance to the Christ child, or to her brother, for that matter. In fact, until we talked about it, Francie did not realize that a divine figure lay behind the astringent person of Elias Tanner, superior court judge.

I urged her to go into the fantasy again, to recover its details in order both to understand and to restore its healing efficacy. Francie paled. "I can't."

"Why not?"

"I don't know. It's scary. It's sick stuff. Masochistic. I'm embarrassed."

I waited. She knew I would not condemn her inner life. In fact, I suspected that for her the way to wholeness lay in reconnecting with the one who had come to salve her childhood wounds, but I did not want to push her too fast, past her healthy self-protective boundaries.

"Well," said Francie, "maybe I could do it here. I'd feel safer with you than by myself."

I nodded. She closed her eyes. I said, "If you say it out loud, I'll write it down. Tell me everything that happens, your feelings, whatever comes up. Don't leave anything out."

She opened her eyes and looked at me, then closed them again. With a wry little twist of her mouth she began.

"I'm on my roller skates, going really fast on the sidewalk when I hit a bump. Some of the sidewalks in my home town had grass growing up between the cracks and I was always running into it and falling, so in my fantasy, that's what I do. I fall headlong. I skin both knees and the heels of my hands, just like last week. I'm lying on the sidewalk wanting to cry when I hear a man's voice. It is *incredibly* kind, and it speaks to me. *Me!* It says, 'Francie!'

"I turn my head and look. It's Mr. Tanner. I'm amazed, because I didn't think he knew me. Now I'm feeling warm all over, especially my chest. . . . My chest is filled, just filled to overflowing with warmth, and even though my body hurts all over I'm soaring, and filled with light. It's so intense I can hardly stand it. He picks me up in his arms and carries me into his office in the courthouse. Then he gets out a first-aid kit and cleans my scrapes and puts iodine on them. It hurts a lot, but he holds me and tells me he's proud of me for being so brave. I feel wonderful, almost a sexual feeling, and he keeps holding me and looking into my eyes and I know everything is going to be all right."

She finished in a rush and opened her eyes with a laugh.

"How do you feel?" I asked.

"A little embarrassed. But good. Really good. Better than I've felt for a long time. Clean and light . . . something lifted off me . . . like everything is going to be all right."

That night she dreamed:

"I am discussing a dream with Janet. The dream within the dream is about the valley of the shadow of death. I think I know the reference, but it is hard to recall the whole thing. I say, 'Yea, though I walk through the valley of the shadow of death . . . ,' then can't remember what is next. It takes a long, long time, but at last something comes to me. I say triumphantly, 'YOU WILL COMFORT ME!' "

The real Mr. Tanner, who became the inner image of her childhood comforter, was a quiet, serious man in his early forties, with black hair and deep brown eyes. She noticed him sometimes when she went to the library near his office. Once, unexpectedly, he spoke to her and she was flooded with warmth. After that, book-loving Francie watched for Mr. Tanner every time she went to the library. As she had once waited for Charles, she now waited for Mr. Tanner, sometimes sitting for hours on the stairs near his office, yearning for a glimpse of him. While she waited, she would stare at the face on a nearby statue of Abraham Lincoln. In time Elias Tanner's kind face merged in her imagination with the face of Lincoln who, she remembered, loved books so much he read at night by firelight.

As time went on, other men replaced Mr. Tanner in the fantasy, but its essential nature remained the same. After she left home and went to college, the outer world claimed Francie back from the spirit that had sustained her, but in a corner of her soul the transcendent one remained intact, waiting to live again.

The day before Christmas Eve, Francie was feeling a lot better, "as if I'd taken a *big shit,*" she said. "I've held it in for too long!" We laughed. It was new for her to use such earthy language. That day she went home with a real smile on her face in place of the pasted-on version to which I had grown accustomed. I offered a silent prayer of thanks to one Elias Tanner, long gone from this world.

It would make a better story if I could say there was a beautiful fall of snow for Christmas, but that is not how it was. The white precipitate did not appear until Twelfth Night, a more fitting time for it anyway. On that day in pagan times, the new light was said to be born and rituals were performed to drive out the evil spirits of the dying year. In the Christian calendar, January 6 is Epiphany, when the divine nature of Christ is made manifest. The freshly falling snow was an epiphany indeed, for "the soul of the commonest object seemed radiant."[11]

However, the heavens made no comment on December 23, when Francie left my office looking like someone reborn. At 4:00 I went out to finish my Christmas shopping. It was already dark, and if the truth be known, Francie's breakthrough was not enough to forestall my annual holiday depression. When I got home, Sean was standing beside the kitchen table. "Behold the risen pelican," he said. I put down my packages and stared. Restored, the creature was splendid, more beautiful than it had ever been. A few shards were missing, ground into dust, and the bird was crisscrossed with cracks. By filling the fissures with Mexican clay, Sean had made the piece appear sculpted from some rare blue marble with earth-red veins. A profu-

---

[11] James Joyce's words. See under "epiphany" in William Rose Benet, *The Reader's Encyclopedia,* 2nd ed. (New York: Thomas Y. Crowell, 1965).

sion of red on the bird's neck and breast looked like blood.

I was stunned. "Do you know the folklore about pelicans?"

Sean shook his head.

"The pelican is supposed to bring its young back to life by plucking out its own breast feathers and sprinkling the dead babies with its blood. It's like an allegory of Christ."

Sean's eyebrows went up but he was silent. I went on, "I wonder why such extraordinary myths have gathered around those birds? Maybe because they look like something from outer space, or maybe it's their ceremonial behavior that touches the imagination. The alchemists had a vessel called a pelican. They said it resurrected the dying. I imagine they meant dying spiritually, but they didn't say so. The alchemical pelican was for distilling fluid, but instead of collecting the stuff in another vessel, it fed the distillate back into its own belly. Jung says that's a symbol for the transformation process. First you distill insight from your experience, then you feed it back into the belly of your unconscious, and it keeps going round and round, getting more and more refined. The alchemists called the process *circulatio.* Edinger says *circulatio,* distilling and coagulating things over and over again, helps bring the opposites together. You know, like good and evil. Usually we separate them by claiming the good stuff for ourselves and seeing the evil in other people, but the pelican brings the whole thing back inside."

Sean nodded. He was putting away the bucket that had held the pelican's pieces. I realized I had gone into professor mode, and wondered if Sean had stopped listening. I was not so sure I understood what I was talking about, anyway, so I could hardly blame him if he tuned me out.

That night Sean dreamed he had the pieces of a man in a bucket. Even though the man was dismembered, he could speak and had not lost his sense of humor. He and Sean had a long talk.

On Christmas day we crowned the pelican with eighteen candles, held by the reeds of his ceramic environment. "Oh Pelican," we said, "Sacred blue Pelican, Pelican risen from the dead, how beautiful you are." Then we lighted him.

After we opened our presents, a little bird with soft brown feathers and a breast and head that glowed with red came to the feeder outside the kitchen window. Honest to God. Sean said it was in the woods the week before, but I had never seen its like. It sat there until it had eaten its fill, a tiny echo of the resurrected icon blazing inside.

4
Saturday's Child

When an archetype is unconsciously constellated and not consciously understood, one is *possessed by it* and forced to its fatal goal.
—Jung, *Letters.*

When I heard the shot, I quit wrestling with the unfamiliar lock and looked up and down the street. My head was throbbing. For three overfull days, I had interviewed San Francisco training candidates, trying to predict whether they would be good Jungian analysts. My judgments, based on interviews no longer than an hour each, would affect those people for the rest of their lives. Now I felt sick, burdened by more responsibility and power than I was ready to carry.

The suburban street was empty. Wondering if my mind had invented the sharp, clear sound of a gunshot, I turned back to the lock on the door of my borrowed apartment. When at last it opened, I glanced at my watch. It was 9:20.

I slept until almost noon the next day, and flew home to Los Angeles that evening. There was a taped telephone message from my friend Katie in Bakersfield. Something in her voice prompted me to call right away.

"A terrible thing happened last night," she said, and stopped. My stomach lurched, fantasy filling the silence. Katie was crying. Finally she went on. "Ilana Tabari—Marge's daughter—was killed."

It was nothing I would have guessed. Remembering twenty-one-year-old Ilana's passion for climbing mountains, I imagined a small female figure slipping over the edge of a precipice and tumbling slowly to the rocks below.

"I was afraid something like that was going to happen," I said. "She was taking such crazy chances. Where was the accident?"

This time the silence was longer. When Katie found her voice, it was hard, controlled. "It wasn't an accident, Janet. Her boyfriend murdered her. She went to his place to break up with him and he shot her. Then he committed suicide."

Stunned, I sat down on the kitchen floor. Katie went on. "When Ilana didn't come home last night, Marge called the police. They broke the lock on Steve's door and let her in. There was blood all over the place, and the bodies, and . . ." She hesitated, then went on in a rush, "There was something really bizarre. A dog was chained in the bathtub, yapping its head off. The police said the inside of the tub was covered with shit, like the dog had been in there for days. The guy must have been nuts."

Of course he was. If he had been sane, he wouldn't have killed her. My mind careened from one thing to the next. I recalled the shot I had heard the day before, and asked Katie for the time of the murder.

"They don't really know. Some time last night. Between eight and midnight I think they said."

My emotions were paralyzed, but the cold, scientific part of my mind toyed with unanswerable questions. Was there some way, psychically, that I could have actually "heard" the shot that killed Ilana? Or was it a coincidence that I thought I heard a shot in San Francisco the night a woman I hardly knew was killed in Bakersfield? The crucial questions did not come to plague me until later. At the time of the murder Ilana's mother, who lived with her daughter and had a close bond with her, was not aware of anything unusual. Why was I the one who heard a shot? If the events in San Francisco and Bakersfield were linked, what were the threads of meaning that connected a middle-aged analyst with a beautiful young woman, killed by her jilted lover?

I turn the pages of my 1981 appointment book until I come upon the August weekend that I spent in San Francisco. I cannot find the time of Ilana's funeral. I was sick that day, I recall. Consciously, I intended to go to the service, but unconscious reactions over which I had no control made me sick and nailed me to the bed. I do not remember doing it, but imagine that I erased the funeral from my calendar in a desperate attempt to go on as if it had never happened.

Slowly I leaf back through the weeks. Her name leaps from the book as if it were written in fire. Ilana Tabari came to my office on Tuesday, June 30, at 1:00 in the afternoon, not six weeks before she was murdered.

Today, eight years later, I can still almost taste the mood of that hour. The new, young patient was vibrating like a high-tension wire after her long drive on the freeway. I offered her a cup of tea and invited her to sit on the couch. "What brings you here, Ilana?"

In a high-pitched, childlike voice, she told me she had come because her mother was worried about her. She went on without waiting for my response, light, cheerful chatter without direction, as if she felt compelled to entertain me. Her opaque brown eyes rarely lighted on my face and she seemed distracted, barely present in the room with me.

Katie had introduced me to Ilana's mother at a party the year before. With shining eyes, Marge had talked of nothing but her daughter, obviously the apple of her eye. Now, meeting the youngster for the first time, I was startled to see how opposite she was to her slow-moving, earthy mother. Ilana was as elusive as quicksilver.

Irritated, I thought, "I wish she'd settle down long enough for me to ask some questions." Then: "God, she's gorgeous! No wonder Marge adores her. She looks like a goddess."

The daughter of a black mother and a Middle Eastern father, Ilana was like an exotic flower. Soft ringlets of long, black hair framed her delicate oval face with its high cheekbones, full lips and almond-shaped eyes. The trace of a limp only underscored the grace with which she moved. She had not yet grown up to her beauty, and I imagine it must have made problems for her. How can someone so young cope with the world's response to such loveliness?

I took a deep breath and interrupted her. "Ilana, do you remember your dreams?"

"Sometimes. Last year I had a super dream about . . ."

Again I broke in, knowing that what she had dreamed the night before would be more germane to her present situation than last year's epic, no matter how memorable. "Please tell me what you dreamed last night."

"Not much, but last year . . ."

"Never mind how little it is. I want to hear what you remember from last night."

She came to rest at last, reaching into her mind to bring what was there into the light. "It isn't much," she said reluctantly, as if offering me an inadequate gift.

"That's fine. Just tell me what you remember."

"Ginger was crying. She's my horse. I've had her since I was a little girl. She was standing there looking at me and crying. That's all I remember."

"Do you mean she was whinnying, making horse noises?"

"No, she was crying. Tears came out of her eyes."

When I finally got the picture, I felt chilled. The strangeness of the image was like an exclamation point that said, "Pay careful attention. The natural order has been disturbed." Something was wrong enough to make the horse that had been Ilana's companion since childhood cry human tears. She might not know it consciously, but an instinct deep within her felt that something was amiss.

Writing about the psychological meaning of fairy-tales, Marie-Louise von Franz has pointed out that the guidance of a helpful animal is the only reliable compass for a hero who faces the problem of evil:

> Though . . . all attempts to deduce a fairy tale morality end in utter paradox, there is *one exception: Anyone who earns the gratitude of animals, or whom they help for any reason, invariably wins out. This is the only unfailing rule that I have been able to find.* It is psychologically of the utmost importance, because it means that in the conflict between good and evil the decisive factor is our animal instinct, or perhaps better, the animal soul.[12]

---

[12] "The Problem of Evil in Fairy Tales," in The Curatorium of the C. G Jung Institute, Zurich, ed., *Evil* (Evanston, IL: Northwestern University Press, 1967), p. 102.

"Why do you think Ginger was crying?" I asked Ilana.

She shrugged.

I pressed her. "Don't think too hard about it. I only want you to try to imagine why."

A shadow passed over her face. She uncrossed her legs, then crossed them again.

"Why, Ilana?"

She sighed. "I guess it's about Steve's dog. My boyfriend. He's kind of cruel to his dog."

"How do you mean?"

She frowned. "It's nothing, really. . . . Sometimes he calls her dirty names. And he puts her in the bathtub when he goes away. He doesn't want a mess all over the house, so he ties her in the tub. She has to go to the toilet there and get it all over herself . . ." Embarrassed, she stopped and scanned my face.

I love animals, and what Ilana was saying disturbed me more than I wanted her to know. Today a growing body of evidence links the abuse of animals to criminal violence,[13] but at the time I was unaware of the connection. I only knew that I felt acutely uncomfortable. "What about you?" I asked. "Does he treat you badly, too?"

She hesitated for a long time before she shook her head.

"What were you thinking?"

"Oh, nothing much. We went mountain climbing last month. He wasn't exactly mean, but . . ."

"But what?"

She told me the story. It is hard to describe the quality of the telling, as if she were neither in the room with me nor on the mountain with Steve where the thing had happened, but floating somewhere else, in a place where none of it mattered.

They were backpacking in the high Sierra. The last day, they got a late start on the most difficult climb of all. It was almost noon before they reached the base of the great granite dome . . .

---

13 A. Felthous, "Aggression Against Cats, Dogs and People," *Child Psychiatry and Human Development,* 1980, pp. 169-177.

The voice of an old friend, a mountaineer, boomed into my mind: *Be off the high peaks by noon.* What else had he said? Something about the sudden Sierra storms. *They're killers. Don't get caught in one on high, exposed rock.*

Ilana was saying that she and Steve had not needed a rope. "There was a fault in the rock that we could follow," she said. "We did it once before, all the way to the top. But this time there was a storm. A big one. Heavy rain, and lots of thunder."

An experienced climber, she told Steve she wanted to go back. "He wouldn't let me," she said.

"What do you mean, 'he wouldn't let you?' Did he use force?"

"Well, no." Her forehead wrinkled. "He just . . . he kept yelling to go higher . . . higher . . ." She shifted in her seat. "He wanted to get to the top."

"And you did what he said."

"I tried to. I wasn't afraid, so I kept going. But I didn't make it." Her voice was unsteady. "I couldn't see. With all the rain. And the lightning. I couldn't see to find a handhold."

Every flash of lightning left an afterimage. She could not find the crevice to brace herself against the wind. A sudden gust lifted, then dropped her. She slid, faster and faster down the dome's increasing steepness until, miraculously, she stopped herself, scrambling on all fours against the momentum of the fall. Her wrist was sprained, knees lacerated, but she was alive.

"You were lucky, Ilana," I said. "Not everyone who does what you did gets a second chance. Do you know how dangerous it is to be on a peak like that in a thunderstorm?"

"I *tried* to tell him."

"But you went along, even though you knew better. Why?"

"I was sure we'd be ok. It felt good to keep going." She looked out the window, watching some people who were walking past. After they turned the corner, she said, "I suppose I was afraid not to do what Steve told me to."

"Why? What did you imagine he would do?"

She shrugged.

I believed I understood. Even at more than twice her age, whenever I was with a man I was all too ready to give him the authority, as if I were a child and he a father who could not be disobeyed. Women do that easily. Unsure of who we are, we hesitate to disappoint our men, and become shaped unconsciously by their images of us.

However, Ilana could not afford that attitude. It had already endangered her life. "Do you love Steve?" I asked.

She rolled her eyes. "Sometimes. But . . ." Her hands moved helplessly.

"Give it some thought. Something is wrong if the horse inside you is so unhappy. You need to take care of her. Don't stay with Steve unless you love him. The real Steve, with all his faults. The one who abuses his dog."

Whether or not a relationship will stand or fall depends a great deal upon the shadow. To love a person for his virtues is easy, but everyone has shortcomings that are not apt to disappear. What Ilana had told me about Steve's shadow was not acceptable to *me*, but the choice was hers.

I looked at my watch. The session was almost over and I had to make a decision. I did not usually work with anyone under twenty-five, but occasionally made an exception for an early-maturing young person with a gift for self-reflection. Ilana seemed young for her age, however, and self-examination was not her strong point.

There were other things to consider, too.

"Ilana, do you *want* to be in analysis?"

She shrugged. "I guess it would be ok if it's what Mom wants."

"Why don't you go to a therapist in Bakersfield?"

"Mom wants me to see you."

Marge's confidence in me was flattering, but Ilana was at an age when young people need to break parental ties. If she saw me only to please her mother, I would not be likely to help her. Besides, the drive from Bakersfield was more than two hypnotic hours long, over mountains and through dense San Fernando Valley smog. In my mind, I kept seeing Ilana's little sportscar flying past a guardrail and rolling over and over down a mountain slope. Coming to Los Angeles every week—even once a month—would create endless opportunities for an accident. I could not accept her as a patient. It made no sense.

"You don't need to be in analysis yet," I said. "There's plenty of time. Come back in a couple of years if you feel like it."

Her relief was so obvious that I felt I had made the right decision. She sped out the door and was halfway to her car when I called to her. "Ilana . . . be careful. It's a dangerous time for you."

Her laughter rang like a silver bell and her words trailed back, "Yes, I'll be careful. Don't worry."

Six weeks later she was dead.

Intuition's virtues have been widely touted in recent years, but used alone it is as one-sided and limited as any other psychological function. One of its drawbacks is imprecision. Intuition smells *something,* but the specifics are not always clear. The image of Ilana falling to her death gave form to an intuition that I understood too narrowly. Even though she had almost lived it literally, its meaning was much broader. A potent archetype was activated in her life.

Ilana behaved like an innocent, as if she were unaware of evil and its consequences. The root meaning of the word *innocent* is "not hurt," or "untouched by death." When a person is truly untouched, innocence can be its own protection, but someone who is too innocent for her age and experience may attract the evil of which she is unconscious. It is as if she dwells on Olympian slopes from which jealous gods will expel her if she tries to stay too long. Since leaving childhood is always a death of sorts, ordinarily followed by rebirth into greater maturity, I did not foresee the hideous finality of Ilana's fall from the heights. Perhaps the mare Ginger knew, and that is why she wept.

Faced with a sudden and violent death, every thoughtful person who has crossed the victim's path is likely to be plagued by "what ifs." We want to believe that the moment of violence was not inevitable. Personally, an event like this activates my omnipotent rescue fantasies. With the wisdom of hindsight I ask myself, "If I had decided to work with her," or "If I had seen the danger clearly," or "If I had understood the archetype better," could I have saved her? Then I remember my words: "Don't stay with Steve unless you love him," and see the cruel paradox that it was precisely in the attempt to leave him that she died. If we understood ahead of time how danger-ous life can be, perhaps no one would ever leave home.

As I write, two noisy crows in the woods outside my house are teaching their fledgling to fly. They have been at it for three days, and I wonder why it is taking so long. When Sean and I return from a walk, the young crow is in the driveway, halfheartedly flapping its wings. Its parents scream at it to move. It hops slowly along the ground and disappears under the house. I want to lure it out and try to help it, but Sean says that something is wrong and it probably will not survive. Besides, my efforts might make matters worse. I re-member the children I caught last year trying to help a fledgling fly by throwing it repeatedly into the air. Caring can go too far.

The parent crows continue to call all afternoon, watching and waiting for their baby to hop out from its hiding place and begin to fly. Early the next morning they are at it again. I peer into the trees and see that either the young crow has been resurrected or another has emerged from the nest. Above me, an adult crow pecks franti-cally at the dead limb on which it is perched. Chunks of bark fall on my head and drive me back into the house.

Soon the entire crow community is involved in the youngster's education. The din is incredible. By mid-afternoon the fledgling is flying unsteadily from branch to branch.

As I am finishing work for the day I hear a loud noise. I think that someone has thrown a rock at the house, but no one is there. Half an hour later, Sean comes home. He stands outside in the driveway for a long time. I go out and find him cradling a small black body, still warm. He says that whoever killed the young crow was a good shot. It probably felt no pain before it fell.

Hurt and rage rip through me like a chain saw. Hopelessly I call to the screaming birds, trying to reassure them that we wish them no harm. How can they believe me? There are more shots the next day, and the next. Sean and I find three more corpses in the street and know that others have fallen in the woods.

In less than a week the forest is silent. No longer innocent, the remaining members of the crow community have taken their lively conversation elsewhere. I will miss them. They were my friends.

For seven years, Ilana Tabari rarely came into my mind. My son Nick, three years her junior, made his way through the hazards of late adolescence, left home and grew slowly into young manhood. His considerable musical gifts bloomed. A few days before his twenty-fifth birthday, however, I had a dream set in a time when he was still living with me, his last year of high school and the year of Ilana's death:

"Nick is sitting at a table eating breakfast, and I am cooking. He is talking about the weekend he spent camping in the mountains with some of his fellow high-school seniors. I am only half listening. He says that a girl was killed, maybe murdered. The others ran away, but he stayed to take care of the body. There is a silence. Suddenly I grasp what he has told me, and feel its emotional impact. I realize that I have to tell him to go to the police and report what happened. I don't want to do this because I'm afraid they will think he killed the girl and lock him up for the rest of his life, but it must be done."

Many aspects of the dream pointed straight to Ilana, but something blocked my memory of her and the events preceding her death. Unconsciously, I feared that the authorities in my psyche would convict *me* of the murder if I brought it to light. In truth, however, my creative energies, symbolized in the dream by my son, would be locked up until I risked investigating the things I had seen and wanted to forget.

Two months passed. One Saturday in April, I stood watching the birds eating at the feeder outside my kitchen window. The book I had written would be published in less than two weeks and I was thinking about starting another, one that would examine some of the ethical dilemmas with which my profession confronts me.

I noticed that a large piece of suet attached to the bird feeder was loose. At the same moment, a voice in my mind said, "Janet, if you start bringing out the stuff you've been thinking about, you'll have to go into the problem of evil. Are you ready for it?" Just then a crow swooped down, grabbed the whole lump of suet and flew into the woods, cawing triumphantly. I ran outside, shouting and cursing. Damned greedy bird. From its position high in a giant fir, it sat and laughed at me.

Inside, my ruminations continued. In the past, I had found that when I focused on an archetypal topic to write about it, the archetype was often activated in my life. What would happen if I took up the problem of evil? Some lines from *Through the Looking-Glass* went through my head:

> Just then flew down a monstrous crow,
> As black as a tar-barrel;
> Which frightened both the heroes so,
> They quite forgot their quarrel.[14]

Meaningless doggerel? Perhaps, but psychological truth so often hides behind apparent nonsense that I decided to look more closely. Seen symbolically, the verse suggests that an emotional reaction to the powers of darkness can reconcile the opposites at war in the psyche. The appropriate emotion is terror.

"You can't avoid the subject forever," said the voice in my head. "After all, you were born on a Saturday."

I shuddered. According to the nursery rhyme, Saturday's child works hard for a living, but that is a euphemism written for children and does not tell the half of it. Saturday belongs to Saturn, a god connected with blackness, depression, cold, heaviness and death. Sometimes equated with Satan, Saturn calls attention to aspects of life that we think of as evil. Gloomy, taciturn and stubborn, he inter-

---

[14] Lewis Carroll, *Alice in Wonderland together with Through the Looking Glass* (London: Pan Books Ltd., 1947), p. 187.

rupts the light, promoting a wholeness that knows both good and evil.

As a Saturday child, I seem destined to confront dark, unconscious realities that most people prefer to ignore. My personal fate, however, is increasingly linked with the collective fate of the era in which we live, for in a manner of speaking, it is now the last day— the Saturday—of the twentieth century and the eon, a time when Jung believed we would all have to come to terms with evil. In a letter to his friend Adolf Keller, he wrote:

> The drive of the unconscious toward mass murder on a global scale is not exactly a cheering prospect. Transitions between the aeons always seem to have been melancholy and despairing times, as for instance the collapse of the Old Kingdom in Egypt . . . between Taurus and Aries, or the melancholy of the Augustinian age between Aries and Pisces. And now we are moving into Aquarius, of which the Sibylline Books say: . . . Aquarius inflames the savage forces of Lucifer. And we are only at the beginning of the apocalyptic development! Already I am a great-grandfather twice over and see those distant generations growing up who long after we are gone will spend their lives in that darkness. I would accuse myself of senile pessimism did I not know that the H-bomb is lying ready to hand—a fact that unfortunately can no longer be doubted.[15]

A far cry from the naive optimism often associated with New Age thought!

A part of me was fighting to keep Ilana out of consciousness, but something else—something saturnine—conspired to bring her closer. Later that day I went to the Video Mart to look for a VCR movie. A film called *Star 80* all but reached out and grabbed me. When I read the blurb on the cover I was skeptical. It was not the kind of thing I usually enjoy, but the box glowed like a luminous marine animal and I kept coming back to it. Finally I took it home. That evening, Sean and I watched the story of twenty-year-old

---

[15] *C.G. Jung Letters* (Bollingen Series XCV), ed. Gerhard Adler and Aniela Jaffé (Princeton: Princeton University Press, 1973), vol. 2, pp. 229-230.

Dorothy Stratton's brutal murder by her husband Paul Snider, who had induced the beautiful young woman to become part of the *Playboy* stable. Although Stratton's natural modesty made the idea of posing nude repugnant, Snider had an uncanny power over her. Little by little she sacrificed her good instincts to his greed for money and power. When she finally broke the spell and tried to leave him, he tortured and killed her, then shot himself.

The last, bloody scenes came to an end and I turned on the lights. Sean pushed the rewind button. "What a creep!" he said.

I could hardly agree more. Paul Snider was as slimy as they come. But something else was bothering me. Why would an innocent young girl be so ready to go along with him and do what he told her, over and over again, no matter how awful it was?

"Something in her unconscious must have wanted fame and money as much as he did or she would've told him to get lost," I said to Sean. "After all, she had been working in a Dairy Queen since she was fourteen. Who wouldn't be seduced by an easy way out?"

Sean gave me a sharp look. "Come on! Don't try to tell me she was to blame for what he did to her."

"No, no, it's not a question of blame. It's just that. . . . Don't you see? She went to such extremes to please him. . . . They were in it together, somehow. Did he have her under a spell, or what?"

A picture flashed into my mind. One of my cats had caught a mouse earlier that week, and brought it into the house. She was not hungry, and played with her victim before she killed it. Whenever the cat let the mouse go, it would sit and gaze into her eyes with what looked almost like adoration, as if an invisible force field bound the two together. Once captured, the mouse appeared to be a willing partner in the game that would end in its death.

Dorothy acted the same way with Paul. "As if he were a god," I said. "Not a nice sweet light god, but the dark primitive kind that demands human sacrifices."

We talked about it for a long time, trying to see the problem from every angle. We would not find a single way to understand it, for the human psyche has many levels and the interaction between two people is infinitely complex.

One way to explain the phenomenon of falling in love is that a piece of your own unconscious psychology is mirrored in your lover. The technical term for it is projection. If the image of a god is projected, it mesmerizes you. Then you are in thrall to the god reflected in the other, and find yourself doing whatever your lover wants, even if it violates what you know and feel consciously. The power of the god stuns you and you lose your will.

Normally the process runs its course with no more than ordinary difficulties. But Paul Snider was a weak man who got drunk on the superhuman power Dorothy Stratton gave him. The more power he got the more dangerous he became because he had no human ethical values to limit him.

"He must have had so little sense of himself that he felt he would cease to exist if she left him," I said.

"I'd put it a little differently," said Sean. "She was a part of him. Losing her was like losing an arm or leg."

"Yes," I said, "and I imagine it was like that for both of them at first. Neither felt complete without the other. She was so light and innocent and he so dark and tarnished that the *coniunctio* would have been activated between them. The dark god and the light goddess trying to get together."

The archetype of the *coniunctio oppositorum,* the union of opposites, expresses the psyche's drive to be whole. Pictured as Christ and Satan, the opposites of good and evil are enormously split in the collective psyche today, the need to bring them together overwhelming. If you have ever been in love with someone you could not possibly live with, but you could not stay away from him and thought you would die if he left you, then you know how *coniunctio* energy feels. It is like the pull between the poles of a magnet. People in other times and places have called it the longing for God, but now that perspective is rare.

Casually, as if I thought about it every day, I said to Sean, "The same thing happened to someone I knew once. It was a year after the Stratton killing almost to the day. Her name was Ilana Tabari and she was a mountain climber." Then I told him the whole story. It was something I had never told anyone before, least of all myself.

That night I dreamed that the vehicle in which I was riding suddenly came to the edge of a cliff. In order to go on I had to descend a steep vertical incline, undercut so severely that it went back the other way.

The dream alarmed me. Clearly, like Ilana, I was about to "come down," perhaps further or harder than was possible to survive. Whereas she had fallen from the heights, I had to descend beneath the earth. Jung once said, "I live in my deepest hell, and from there I cannot fall any further,"[16] but I had not reached that enviably stable state. I regretted thinking so much about the problem of evil. The topic had picked me, however, not the other way around, and forcing myself to think pleasant thoughts did not seem likely to help. On the contrary.

That week I made an extra effort to notice what was going on, inside and out, and make a few notes in my journal every day. On Monday I wrote: "I'm feeling horrible anxiety, so bad I've been trying to drown it by drinking brandy. What a mistake! Now I'm drunk *and* anxious. Foolish me! I wish Sean were here. Maybe I'll call some people and ask for donations to Tamanawas."

Tamanawas was a fund to finance the efforts of a support group for people in emotional crisis. We worked with patients in their homes, an alternative to the usual hospital treatment for acute psychosis. After several fundraising calls, I felt less agitated.

Tuesday: "I'm scared. I wonder if the compulsion to solicit money for Tamanawas is about *me*. Am I going crazy?"

Wednesday: "I feel better. Maybe I won't go crazy after all. Rosemary called and asked if anything is going on with Tamanawas. Last night she dreamed that someone phoned from a booth at the side of the road and asked for Tamanawas, then hung up. Is she picking up my stuff?"

---

[16] Marie-Louise von Franz, *C. G. Jung: His Myth in Our Time* (New York: C. G. Jung Foundation, 1975), p. 174.

Thursday: "Sean fantasized that an assassin was approaching the house with a gun. He thinks we're too vulnerable here."

When I awoke Friday morning, I was dreaming about a madwoman who had a terrible toothache. I took her to the dentist, then hurried to get some delicious candy—thin sheets of chocolate with bees embedded in it.

The madwoman and her pain gave graphic form to my distress, but what was the meaning of the bee-studded chocolate? I imagined that something like it might have caused the woman's toothache in the first place. Several weeks later I remembered that chocolate is the devil's food, but at the time I did not understand that I was rushing toward Hades like a bee to honey.

I was still in bed and not quite out of the dream when Sean asked if I would like to meet him at an outdoor concert later in the day. I struggled to overcome an irrational conviction that I was going to be busy with something else. Finally I answered, "I don't know. It's an unpredictable day." Puzzled, Sean looked out the window at the sunny sky. I said, "I don't mean the weather." I could not explain what I did mean. That would only be clear later, when the thing I intuited became reality.

It began with a taped telephone message from a therapist in another city. A year later I heard her quoted as an expert on Satanic cults, but when she phoned me, Liz Hunter was a stranger. Her voice came from my answering machine in rapid bursts, like machine-gun fire, punctuated with laughter that belied the grim import of her words: "I understand you have the capacity to contain someone in crisis, and I have a patient in crisis who needs to be contained from tonight until noon tomorrow. It is the anniversary of her daughter's murder. She believes she must die tonight. Please call before 6:00 if you can help."

The peculiar thing is that I never considered saying no. Against all good sense I took the next step, and the next, as if I were under a spell. Not only did I lack the fear that would have been appropriate, an indescribable sense of peace came over me. In retrospect, I believe it was the same sweet calm that some people emanate when they have decided to commit suicide, like the hush at the center of a hurricane. I suppose that what *The Book of Common Prayer* calls "the peace of God that passeth all understanding" always resides in the Great Mystery, even when the form it takes is death. Although I cannot be sure, I imagine that my mood was not so different from Ilana Tabari's as she climbed higher and higher in the storm.

I assumed that Liz's patient was delusional and would need the Tamanawas support group. In time it became clear that my assumption was not correct. Liz believed that Serena's story was literally true, not a crazy fantasy. The "family" who had killed her daughter on this date the year before required Serena to present herself for ritual murder that night. She felt compelled to obey. Liz and a man friend intended to kidnap her to keep her safe, and were looking for a place to hide her until noon the next day.

Tamanawas had no housing for a person from out of town, but I agreed to help anyway. Driven by something in my psyche whose nature I did not understand, I offered a room in my own home, the very place whose vulnerability Sean had mentioned the day before.

"Is her family a Satanic cult?" I asked.

"Maybe. I don't want to talk about it now. They might have this phone tapped."

"What time should we expect to hear from you?"

"She's coming to my office for a 6:00 therapy hour. We'll leave as soon as we can get her into the car, and should be there between nine and ten. Don't tell me your address. I'll call you from a phone booth on the way."

"You did *what?*" said Sean. "The guest room? *Here?*"

I wavered, no longer so sure I had done the right thing. Trying to smile, I said, "I don't think I can get out of it now. They're on their way."

It was a long wait. A fire in the woodstove kept us warm enough, but an uneasy wind disturbed the forest outside, drawing my eyes repeatedly to the dense darkness beyond floor-to-ceiling windows. When Sean stood up I thought he was going to tend the fire, but instead he went to the closet and brought out his bright red backpack. He leaned it against the wall near his chair, taking a long time to arrange it just so. Something in the back of my mind wondered what he was doing, but I did not ask. I was thinking about the car moving toward us through the night.

As we went over and over what had happened, everything outside our small circle of lamplight began to seem unreal. By the time the phone call came it was almost 10:00 and we had stopped believing in it. My conversation with Liz did not help. For one thing, the line kept going dead and she had to keep calling back. For another, her voice seemed changed and the afternoon's nervous laugh had disappeared. I began to doubt that I was talking to the same person.

"Where *are* you?" I asked.

"In a phone booth not far from you, but now we have to go to the hospital in Cape Freeman. They kidnapped Serena and carved her up and probably raped her."

I felt dazed. It did not occur to me to ask how the "family" had kidnapped Serena from a moving car, or how Liz had gotten her back. None of it made sense. Visualizing a dismembered body, I could only repeat stupidly, "carved her up?" A morgue seemed more appropriate than a hospital.

"They carved the cult logo on her chest," snapped Liz.

"Why don't you go to the hospital *here?* Cape Freeman is an hour away."

"Yes, but they have an expert in getting forensic evidence of rape. We'll need it. May we still call you if they discharge her tonight? It will probably be very late, but you're the only safe place we know."

"Sure," I said without missing a beat.

As soon as I put the phone down my mind began to raise questions. "Listen," I said to Sean, "I'm beginning to think this whole thing must be someone's idea of a practical joke. Either that, or this so-called therapist is the crazy one and Serena is only a figment of her insane imagination. The story doesn't hang together. Why would they come all the way here just to turn around and go to Cape Freeman?"

The more we talked about it, the more uncertain we became. At midnight Sean called the police, in case we should need help. Then I rang the emergency room at the hospital in Cape Freeman. "I want to find out if a patient of mine got there safely," I lied. "She was raped and mutilated. She's with a woman named Liz Hunter and . . ."

The medic interrupted me. "They got here all right. A few minutes ago." The awe in his voice told me that what I had heard from Liz was neither joke nor delusion but God's own truth, even though I never heard from Liz again.

At three o'clock we went to bed, and at nine, Rosemary came for breakfast. Between us, Sean and I recounted the night's events. Rosemary reached for a bagel and ate the whole thing, slowly, before she said anything. It gave me a long time to think. When it was all put into words, with each inexorable step following the next, the story sounded dreadful, far more ominous than I had believed.

Rosemary finished her bagel. "Whew!" she said, "I feel as if a big black cloud was headed straight for your house. For some reason, it kept on going and passed you by. You were really lucky."

"Yes," said Sean, "I was pretty worried. Worried enough to bring the magnum over."

I stared at him, my mind moving with the agility of refrigerated honey. Magnum? What was he talking about? Slowly the image oozed into shape and I understood that he was referring to his pistol, the one he ordinarily kept in a drawer at his studio. Was that why he had positioned his backpack so carefully the night before, why he had kept it beside the bed while we slept and why, even now, it was within easy reach of where he sat? Because the magnum was in it?

"In your pack?" I asked.

His nod confirmed it. For the first time I grasped how concerned he had been for our safety. I was suddenly filled with emotion, the thing I had managed not to feel for the last sixteen hours, alarm born of the need for self-protection. My head cleared and the words I had said to Ilana Tabari years before came back to me: *Not everyone who does what you did gets a second chance.* I began to tremble. I had walked into the cult's domain with steps as irrevocable as those that took six million Jews into Hitler's gas ovens. It was as if something deep within me resonated to Serena's predicament. I, too, could have been a human sacrifice. What had possessed me?

In my dream, a handsome and idealistic man of my acquaintance is cooking dinner. I wonder if he has romance in mind and feel uneasy, for I am married to someone else. Wanting to make myself useful, I decide to prepare some tea. I find a drinking glass like the ones I have at home, fill it with a flammable fluid and light it. It glows with a beautiful amber color. It is too hot to hold. I put it down and try to balance the teakettle on it, but the whole thing falls over and the liquid fire is spilled.

The dream confronts me with a problem that I share with others whose spiritual needs are not met by traditional religion. Lacking satisfactory containers for what Jung calls the *numinosum,* the fiery essence of divine power, we overload ordinary human situations like love affairs by projecting God into them. Meeting the *numinosum* in human romance is like lighting a fire in an ordinary drinking glass. Idealism is no substitute for awareness of the consequences. Enacted naively in literal reality, the divine turns demonic.

The dream suggests no solution. Unless an adequate vessel is found, such a fire can become a holocaust. Contained in a religious context a holocaust is a sacred offering, a burnt sacrifice, but the same fire raging out of control in the profane world has produced some of the twentieth century's greatest tragedies.

Soon after the dream, an article in *Time* magazine points to a hot spot of this sort in the world today:

> The words "obsessive fan" cause a premonitory chill among celebrities these days. Increasingly they have seen that the most fervent admirers can turn into crazed attackers. The problem has become more evident since the beginning of the decade, when Mark David Chapman killed John Lennon. . . . There has been a rash of ugly episodes, some murderous, some merely distressing.[17]

---

[17] July 31, 1989.

Experts attribute the phenomenon to unrequited love, but my dream suggests that a larger context may be needed to grasp what at first looks like romance. I imagine that the obsessive fan who kills is possessed by a drama that began with the ancient fertility gods and culminated in the crucifixion. Call it the archetype of the sacrificed god. Because for many people the Christ image is no longer a living symbol, the fire of this archetype is loose in the streets. The high-profile celebrity is a lightning rod for the energy of the sacrificed god. The fan who is gripped by this image and cannot sacrifice his obsession, for instance by understanding and symbolizing it, instead sacrifices the *object* of obsession, the person carrying the god-image.

At bottom, I believe that divine power gone wrong is the key to Ilana Tabari's fate. She is not alone. Think of the Third Reich, a whole nation in thrall to a weak and charismatic man; or the Manson "family," willing even to murder at the command of a hippie with compelling eyes who thought he was Jesus Christ. Consider a respected minister and humanitarian named Jim Jones, somehow transmuted into the self-styled savior who led more than nine hundred mesmerized followers to their death in Guyana.

Who of us has never fallen prey to superhuman power misplaced? Who has not subjugated his own deepest truth to the will of a charismatic leader, agreed to be someone else's savior, unwittingly victimized another, or been a willing sacrificial victim? Who can claim to be immune to the dark side of God?

5
Mirrors of God

When the god is not acknowledged, egomania develops, and out of this mania comes sickness.
—Jung, "Commentary on *The Secret of the Golden Flower.*"

Ruth smoothed her skirt and put the typed page on her lap. She rarely brought dreams to her therapy but when she did, the air crackled. What was it, I wondered? Dread? Anticipation? Or something else? She gave me an enigmatic glance and began to read:

"In my dream I am in the world of anarchists. The scenes are darkly illuminated through tattered curtains, windows high from the ground, dusty, dark and smoky. No one claims his real identity. In the streets below is chaos, debris everywhere. Chunks of cement block the roads, buildings are missing parts of their identities, mixed up in the randomness of the rubble. There is no smell nor sound, little color. Along the edges, crumpled bodies cling to the shadows. Are they alive? It is not important, for they are not one of us.

"We meet in dim, third-world rooms above the silent mayhem. The men are thin, smelling of stale cigarette smoke, the harsh acrid kind, cheap, from Europe or the Middle East. I try to attract/attach myself to one of the tall, powerful leaders. He is quiet, rarely speaking. How does he lead? What is the mission? There is no sound. I feel powerless/all-powerful, choosing to ride along others' paths, not planning my own."

Hoping my face did not betray the shock and pain the desolate images touched in me, I struggled to reconcile the vital appearance of this striking, well-dressed woman with the picture the dream painted. For the first time I saw that she was devastated inside, holding herself together by an act of will. Although seven years had passed since she defected, chaos and desolation continued to dog her. As it

71

once had been in the group, so it was now in her colorless inner world, where she had no identity of her own, no power except the reflected glory to be attained by attaching herself to the all-powerful leader, the guru. Barren and chaotic as this place was, it would be worse not to to be part of it, for outsiders were as good as dead.

Together we looked up the word *anarchy* and traced it to its root meaning, "without a ruler," noting its most general definition: "absence of any cohering principle, as a common standard or purpose." Lacking a living connection to either a religious tradition or the authority in the psyche that Jung called the Self, Ruth's life was formless. In the depths of her psyche, however, something hungered for order and meaning and, like the medieval soul blindly seeking God, she searched restlessly for a master.

At forty, Ruth was as vulnerable as she had been twenty-three years before, when she met Christine Welter, the group's charismatic leader. Later the eminent Dr. Welter lost her license, but then no one suspected there might be cause. On the contrary. Ruth's mother could afford the best, and had sent her young daughter to a therapist whose original ideas, regal bearing and hypnotic black eyes commanded the respect of famous and forward-looking people all over the world.

Christine had not been the one who told Ruth about the inner circle of "special" patients.

"Who, then?" I asked.

Ruth slowly shook her head, forehead furrowed beneath a shock of prematurely-white hair. "I'm not sure. Maybe Frank. I ran into him in the waiting room one day when Christine got her schedule mixed up, and somehow we wound up having coffee together. He didn't say much about the group. Just enough to make me curious. Later he introduced me to some of the others. I longed to be part of it, but Christine told me I wasn't ready. She said I was too sick. By the time she let me join, I wanted it more than anything in the world. I had arrived." Ruth's laugh was bitter.

The control over her life came gradually. Accustomed to having her mother and even her brothers and sisters tell her what to do, the girl hardly noticed. Christine urged her to become a physician and she complied without question, turning away from aesthetic gifts that expressed a deeper inclination. Instead of going to art school, she dutifully lived out an unfulfilled side of her therapist, who felt at a disadvantage in her chosen field without a medical degree.

Christine managed the sex lives of everyone in the group, while helping herself freely to all the men and many of the women. She persuaded Ruth to leave home and move in with another group member, a lesbian woman who became sexually obsessed with her. For a time Ruth imagined she must be gay, even though she was not at all attracted to her new roommate. After she turned twenty-one, however, her therapist gave her a sixteen-year-old boy to initiate sexually. Ruth fell in love with him and the boy was hastily reassigned. Love was not a part of Christine's plan, and she now encouraged Ruth to immerse herself in the orgies that had become a weekly practice of the group.

Eventually everyone in the group was subjected to drug experiments, ostensibly for therapeutic reasons. Ruth recalled the drug sessions with horror, particularly one in which she was given the anesthetic ketamine. According to Goodman and Gilman, ketamine produces "dissociative anesthesia," so-called because it makes one feel dissociated from the environment. "Purposeless movements sometimes occur, and occasionally violent and irrational responses to stimuli are observed." Awakening from the drug state "is not infrequently characterized by disagreeable dreams and even hallucinations. Sometimes these unpleasant occurrences may recur days or weeks later. Almost half of adults over the age of 30 years exhibit delirium or excitement, or experience visual disturbances."[18]

Ketamine shattered Ruth's personality. In a hallucination induced by the drug, she sat among jagged shards, trying futilely to piece herself back together. Years later she wrote: "Oh God, how can I hang onto my boundaries when the drugs are destined to tear them

---

[18] *The Pharmacological Basis of Therapeutics* (New York: Macmillan, 1985), p. 298.

away. Where can I hide my privacy? It is all right, isn't it, to have a private self, if it is not demented? Aren't the ones who are called crazy really only wearing private selves? What was I trying to do, blow myself off the planet? What a price I have paid for a shortcut to Nirvana!"

Not long after permitting Ruth to join the group, her therapist convinced her to use money inherited from her father to buy a collective residence. By bringing celebrities to the house from every field of cultural endeavor, Christine provided a lively and self-contained intellectual life. In time there were group members from most of the major businesses and professions. Contact with the outside world, with those who were "not one of us," became superfluous. Like an incestuous family, the group satisfied every need. Outsiders were viewed with suspicion or downright hostility.

As Christine's bizarre domination grew more and more extreme, Ruth began to see that something was wrong. But she had known nothing else for twelve long years, her entire adult life. How could she possibly leave? Eventually she married a man who was not in the group, he supported her growing doubts, and they fled together to another state.

In the ensuing years, Ruth was consumed with shame. It cut both ways. When she looked at herself through the eyes of the outside world, she was ashamed of the horrors in which she had taken part. As an influential group member who eventually shared the leadership, she could not blame Christine alone for abuses of sex, drugs and power with which she herself had cooperated. From the other side, she felt ashamed of her disloyalty to Christine and the group. The people she once had counted as friends now shunned her. Perhaps she would never recover from the subtle conviction of failure, the irrational suspicion that something was wrong with her because she could no longer comply.

The night that Ruth dreamed of the anarchists, I, too, had a dream whose central image hinted at a paradoxical equivalence between power and powerlessness.

"I enter a monastery or convent at the top of a hill and try to find my way through its rooms and floors. In one room, crowds of people are gathering to hear a lecture by an East Indian guru. I decide not to attend because I have heard him before and was not impressed, but a friend rushes past and says, 'You should hear this man. He's wonderful!' Thinking that perhaps I have misjudged him, I find a seat where I can listen. The guru, a brown and shriveled old man who apparently cannot use his legs, is carried in by several of his disciples. The crowd applauds and cheers and he begins to speak. I listen carefully, but he is only saying meaningless words that appear to mesmerize the audience. I stay for a few minutes to be sure, then quietly make my way through the crowd and out the door."

The coincidence in time between my dream and Ruth's made me aware that the archetype of the guru or cult leader was activated between us. Considering her tendency to gain the illusion of power by attaching herself to a powerful leader, I would have to be very careful. She needed to find her authority within, by attending to her long-abandoned inner life, but she could all too easily give it to me. It would be equally easy for me to accept the projected role unless, as in my dream, I consciously turned away from the guru in my psyche. The dream warned me clearly that if I agreed to be a guru I would lose the use of my legs.

A colleague once suggested that analysts are lazy people who are motivated to do their own inner work by the need to keep up with their patients. So it was that Ruth brought me face to face with a part of myself and my life that I might otherwise have buried forever. I imagine I recall so little about the Danny Silverman affair because I do not like to think of myself as the kind of woman who would run away to South America with a man she met through an ad in the newspaper, but there it is. The way I *want* to think of myself, Jung would say, butters no parsnips. How could I have been so naive? I must have been under a spell.

Danny was an animus-man, a dangerously fascinating sort of *homme fatal*. Much has been said about the anima-woman, who does not have a mind of her own but takes on the identity of her man's anima, his unconscious feminine side. If she is unscrupulous, she can destroy a man. Her male counterpart, whose power to enact a woman's secret fantasies is equally alluring, has been given less attention. Lacking authentic inner strength, the animus-man embodies the unconscious images of whatever woman he happens to be with. If he has a touch of psychopathy, he can be deadly.

Danny had a Jewish name and dressed like an exile from the Ivy League, but he had lived for a time in Trinidad and had a distinctly Caribbean flavor. I remember him dancing about the bedroom wearing a bright yellow towel that showed off his deeply-tanned skin. He was talking about *Finnegan's Wake,* all the while bumping and grinding like a native boy and a girl from the Folies Bergères rolled into one.

I was enchanted. I can hardly believe the whole thing lasted less than two months in real time, for subjectively, years passed. At first we searched for a house where we could live together, then Danny began to talk about South America. I was seized by the fantasy of a journey into the unknown, an expedition that I did not realize I needed to take internally instead, deeper than I had hitherto gone into the jungle of my own psyche.

Since the *coniunctio* was activated between us, steamy sexual images dominate my memories of Danny. One blazing Sunday afternoon he took me to swim at the home of his former wife. I assumed she would be out, and was not exactly pleased to find the wife lying by the pool, dressed only in a cynical smile. Danny took off his clothes and invited me to do likewise. I clung to my swim suit. The sexual energy was as torrid as the day, but I was too naive to realize that the woman's presence was not accidental. For her part, I imagine she did not like my looks. Danny never took me there again.

The days passed like a feverish dream. Evenings with Danny rarely began before ten p.m. because I was seeing forty or more patients every week, directing the analyst-training program at the Jung Institute, teaching, and serving on several professional committees. I cannot have been aware that I was mortal, for I left no space in my schedule for basic human needs.

Just as Danny was molded by my projections, unconscious fantasies at work in my professional community controlled the shape of my life. Almost as soon as I finished my training I had become mysteriously attractive as an analyst, teacher, and potential leader. It did not occur to me to refuse excessive demands on my time and energy, for they satisfied my desire to be wanted. My spiritual needs and those of my community fit together like a lock and key. I burned with idealistic fervor, longing to sacrifice my life to something larger than myself. They were looking for a savior and thought they had found one. That was when I lost my legs, my standpoint on the ground of ordinary human reality. For all practical purposes I became a guru. Alas, popularity exceeded professional competence, for my work was still unseasoned. Otherwise I might have seen that something was wrong.

Much as a child's psyche is marked by the unconscious psychology of the family into which she is born, mine had been stamped by the graduate program where I first studied clinical psychology. It was an intimate department, its faculty drawn almost exclusively from its former students. This small community of devoted individuals provided a benevolent and nurturant container for my spiritual needs, feeding a hunger of which I was only marginally aware. Although I did not know it, we were very like a cult.

Julian Weiss, the department's original chairman, was getting on in years and was nominally retired. He still had extraordinary power, however, partly because he had once been therapist to most of the men and women on the faculty. He came to his office daily and worked diligently to propagate his particular approach to psychology, an eclectic blend of clinical theory, psychoanalysis and Jewish mysticism. Displayed prominently on his wall was an astonishing photograph of Sigmund Freud wearing a yarmulke, the skullcap of the Orthodox Jew.

Julian had as a role model the *zaddik*, the Just Man of Jewish tradition. This exalted figure embodies an ideal of moral, social and religious perfection that entitles him to a position of spiritual authority akin to the guru's in the Far East. Like most cult leaders, Julian was intolerant of dissent and nursed fantasies of immortality. I will never forget the talk I had with him when, as a student, I was asked to take over some minor departmental responsibilities. He spoke at length of his hope that I would preserve his version of psychology's true spirit. Referring to those who did not share his perspective, he hissed, "They don't understand what it's about. They're just waiting for me to die so they can do it *their* way. But I'm going to fool them. I'm not *going* to die." He stared at me with glittering eyes.

He was not joking and I was terrified. For a long time I had regarded Julian with affection and amusement as the original bionic man, because he replaced body parts as fast as they wore out. I knew he was one of technology's wonders, from his stainless steel hip joints to the plastic lens in his left eye and the pacemaker that prompted his slowing heart, but I had not guessed what a serious game he was playing. For many years I could not accept that this man who had touched my life in crucial, perhaps even lifesaving ways had fallen victim to one of the biggest pitfalls for any therapist whose work goes deep. He had become identified with God.

Fate was kinder to me. I traveled only a short way along the road to immortality before sickness leveled me. It began the day that Danny Silverman tried to take a pair of scissors to my hair without permission. Something in me rose up and said no to his fantasies for the first time, and I angrily refused to let him cut me into the pattern of his ideal woman. Within hours, my temperature climbed to 103. I remembered reading in an unpublished seminar of Jung's that sickness is the body's way of relieving an overloaded psyche. Do not deplore sickness, he said, but be grateful to the body for helping to carry your burden. Although it would be years before I understood, I *was* grateful. With enormous relief I resigned from all responsibilities and sank into bed. After a week of cooking my meals, Danny left without a word and never came back. I did not try to call him, for by now I understood that a mortal woman was not what he wanted.

It was weeks before the mysterious burning in my body was diagnosed, months before I recovered. The cytomegalo (large-celled) virus that had invaded my liver—ancient seat of life and the soul—

was a precise physical analogy of the thing that inflamed my psyche, driving me to be bigger than I could.

"Have I ever told you about the time I almost moved to South America?" I asked Sean.

An incredulous look crossed his face. I went on. "It was a crazy time. I came very close to moving to Guyana with a man I hardly knew."

Sean gave a long, slow whistle. "Jonestown?"

"I don't know. For some reason, I never asked exactly where he had in mind. It *was* 1978, though. If we had gone to Jonestown, we would have gotten there just in time for cyanide-flavored Koolade."

Sean walked across the room and sat down in the rocker. It creaked back and forth, back and forth. When he spoke, his voice was muffled behind his hand. "What stopped you?"

"Dumb luck," I said. "I got sick."

The rocker creaked faster. Sean was staring out the window. Finally he said, "I guess that was before Theodore."

I gave him a hard look. Didn't he realize that Theodore had been my therapist, not a lover? Still, the connection struck a nerve. Theodore was different from Danny, but they were both animus-men. I went to the bookshelf and leafed through the black-bound volumes of Jung's *Collected Works* until I found what I was looking for. "Listen to this," I said. "You'd think that Jung knew Theodore personally. I couldn't describe him better myself!"

Not every man of real intellectual power can be an animus, for the animus must be a master not so much of fine ideas as of fine words—words seemingly full of meaning which purport to leave a great deal unsaid. He must belong to the "misunderstood" class, or be in some way at odds with his environment, so that the idea of self-sacrifice can insinuate itself. He must be a rather questionable hero, a man with possibilities.[19]

---

[19] "Marriage as a Psychological Relationship," *The Development of Personality*, CW 17, par. 339.

Sean laughed. Musing, I returned the book to the shelf. For years I had struggled to understand how I could have given myself away so completely to a man who, with hindsight, I found it hard to respect. Now I saw that Theodore had actually said and done very little to warrant the godlike things my imagination ascribed to him. It was only that he rarely said *anything* clearly. Like the characters in Ruth's anarchy dream he did not claim his real identity. It was easy to project almost anything into him and, in the aftermath of the illness that drove Danny away, I did.

Giving my authority to Theodore was a gradual process, not unlike what happens in brainwashing. Having been deposed, by the grace of God, from the status of near-idol, I was depressed and vulnerable, my self-confidence so badly shaken that I was a sitting duck for any charismatic person who would tell me what to do. In this frame of mind I asked Theodore, a former student and devotee of Julian Weiss, to be my therapist. It was as if something drove me to play the guru-disciple game until I either understood it or perished in its fire. From the guru position I moved to that of true disciple, suppressing my own feelings and reactions again and again until, like Ruth, I was powerless/all powerful, riding along Theodore's plans, not planning my own. When I finally saw my mentor's all-too-human frailty I could not accept it, and the guru-disciple bond blew apart like a nuclear bomb. I floundered for several years, trying to put myself back together and contemplating suicide because Theodore and the intimate circle of his followers now behaved as if I were invisible. All the while the image of God danced on his face and I felt that without his approval I might as well be dead. I was overwhelmed with shame and, like Ruth, told no one what had happened for several years.

Ruth's face contorted with pain. "How could I have been so blind? Things got more and more horrible and I didn't leave, couldn't even think about leaving. What was the matter with me?"

It was hard to let her have all that guilt. "You were just a child," I said. "And she was your therapist. How could you know?"

"Yes, but somewhere inside I *did* know. Not right away, but as time went on I could see that something was terribly wrong. I kept telling myself the bad things were exceptions."

Suddenly I saw how easy it would be to deprive her of her inner strength as surely as Christine had. If I tried to quiet the authoritative voice within her that insisted she be responsible for her actions, however unconscious, I would usurp the role of a personal savior, taking Ruth's sins upon myself and separating her from the God within. My role was not to save her from herself but the contrary, to help her understand and relate to whatever was in her.

I had to take her question seriously. What *did* make her so susceptible to Christine's domination, powerless but at the same time infinitely powerful by virtue of her connection to the charismatic woman? Was it merely a matter of being in the wrong place at the wrong time, an unfortunate accident of fate? Or was *she* part of it? We examined a number of factors, any one of which could have been decisive.

When she came to Christine, Ruth was aflame with the idealism of late adolescence, when altruism and spiritual feelings lie close to the surface. She was ready and eager to give herself to something larger. Had her therapist understood it, the impulse might have energized a process of inner growth and transformation that would eventually take her far beyond herself. But instead, Ruth's religious feelings were externalized and became stuck, fixed on Christine and the group.

There was something else, too. Ruth was a twin. Since her brother was delivered ahead of her, we speculated that the tendency to follow another was imprinted on her psyche at birth. When her twin was not there, she was driven compulsively to find another person to fill the empty space, an inclination supported by our culture's extraversion.

Even though they were not identical twins, Ruth and her brother thought and did similar things at similar times. No words had to be spoken for each to know what was going on in the other. In Ruth, this intuitive mode of knowing another's innermost thoughts and feelings grew into an exquisite sensitivity. By the time I met her she had a highly-developed gift for seeing and meeting others' needs, even before they themselves knew such a need existed.

Growing up with a narcissistic mother sharpened her intuitive gift to a fine point. In Ruth's memory, her mother was constantly in front of a mirror, dressing herself or putting on makeup, the little girl silent in the background, fascinated, endlessly watching. The mother had no idea that Ruth was a separate person. She hardly noticed the child at all but when she did, it was as if she were an extension of herself. Thus, her only living parent strengthened Ruth's role as the second-born twin. Unconsciously she trained the child never to put herself first. Ruth learned to suppress her feelings and reactions until she no longer knew what they were, and was left without internal ground or direction. She dreamed:

"I am a ship without a rudder. A large ship, one of those high-riding container ships that look like shoe boxes atop the water. When they go by from a distance they look uninhabited. Am I the ship or the only passenger? No one is around. Again there is no sound. The colors are variations of grey, from olive drab green to cold hard steel blue. The light is eerie, a sulphurous phosphorescent. Power is an issue. Is there any? I cannot hear the engines. Without a rudder, how can you claim a direction?"

At an earlier time, the church might have offered a safe and predictable connection to God as a way to steer her ship. Today, however, she is caught in the same alienated boat as others for whom traditional religious forms do not quite work. This is the meaning of Nietzsche's 100-year-old declaration that God is dead. In truth divine power, the archetypal energy to which we give the name of God, is very much alive, and we stumble across it in unexpected places, often at our peril.

Perhaps the proliferation of cultlike groups in the contemporary Western world results from the psyche's effort to create new containers for the living spirit, vessels in which to transform the suffering caused by the abuse, neglect, narcissism and just plain human imperfection in our original families. Unfortunately, few groups or their leaders are up to this enormous spiritual task. In the Far East the guru system appears to work, but here something always seems to go awry when the members of a group unanimously invest absolute authority in one individual. Because the dark side of the godhead is presently activated in the collective unconscious, pressing to be re-united with its all-good opposite, any human being who becomes a mirror for the God-images of a cult-like following perforce must wrestle with the Satanic aspects of divine status.

As Ruth's dream suggests, the issue has to do with power and its locus. Unless a cult leader is more conscious than most humans can be, with the ethical sensibilities of a saint, he will sooner or later succumb to identification with divine power and try to live it out in the world of profane reality. Literalized, spiritual power becomes excessive material power and/or wealth, and union with God is reduced to personal sexual license. Such inappropriate personal power would be cut off at its source if cult members were to develop individual relationships with the God within. Then the Christines and Theodores and Julians of the world, to say nothing of the James Joneses and Charles Mansons and Hitlers, would be delivered from tragic fates.

Ruth's involvement with the archetype of power was initially as a follower. Later, especially after her family medical practice became successful, her extraordinary capacity to meet others' needs put her at risk in a different way. As she had given divine authority to Christine, others now offered it to her. At this juncture, her role as the second-born twin protected her, for she was wary of accepting power over others. If she did, the terrible grip of archetypal power would cause her to lose herself to her following as surely as she had to Christine.

As I write, the Berlin Wall is coming down. All over Europe, pieces of the iron curtain are being cut up and sold as souvenirs. Surging seas of humanity renounce totalitarianism and claim the right to personal freedom. Petty tyrants who have killed thousands in cold blood are themselves hunted down, ridiculed, humiliated, tortured and executed. Perceiving the euphoria and divine vengeance that echo in the subterranean chambers of my own psyche, I feel a chill of fear. Are we ready for an undivided world?

Sean and I have been watching a series of documentaries about the Third Reich.[20] We see enthusiastic masses of healthy-looking people gripped by something like religious fervor. Their conviction of absolute rightness and righteousness causes them to move as one. An anxious-looking little man named Hitler, too small for his clothes, is transformed before our eyes, appearing to grow physically larger as public adulation pumps him up like a blimp.

I listen carefully to interviews with ordinary citizens who dared to resist and survived to tell about it. I want to know if it is possible to defy archetypal power without getting caught by it, either martyred or possessed by the very thing opposed in others. The stories of two self-assured women are enlightening. Neither was naive about the malignant power of the SS men she confronted, and both were able to trick their antagonists. One used her knowledge of the law and of Hitler's words to suggest, in subtle ways, that she had more power than they and could make trouble for them. The other lied, repeatedly, consistently and convincingly. She felt bad about lying so much, she said, but quoted the words of a friend: "What is freedom? Freedom means you are not forced to lie."

Since I was born only days after Hitler became Fuhrer of the Third Reich, my psyche was touched by the Nazi problem at its inception. One of the earliest photographs of me shows an adorable little girl wearing a dress, a hair ribbon, booties, and an engaging little smile. I am propped up on a couch or chair, and my right arm is raised awkwardly over my head and forward with the hand palm down. For years I was led to believe that I was waving good-bye, but near the end of her life my mother admitted that my father had taught me the Nazi salute. "We all thought Hitler was a savior," she said.

Sean asks me if I remember how, in the late thirties and early forties, we used to do the salute to the flag. I remember all right. The

---

20 "The Third Reich," Thames Television Ltd., 1975.

first thing every morning, we school-children were all required to stand very straight, put our hands on our hearts, face the flag at the front of the room and say in unison, "I pledge allegiance to the . . ."

At the word "flag," we all extended our arms upward and out toward the flag, hands palm down, and kept them there until we finished.

Sometime after the United States entered World War II, it changed and we had to learn to keep our hands on our hearts all the way through.

I look at Sean. "Do you suppose . . . ?"

"Yes," he says. "I kept wondering why it changed so suddenly. Finally I asked my parents and they told me it was because of the Nazi salute."

In 1938, Jung discussed Hitler's psychology in a remarkable interview by H. R. Knickerbocker. Stalin and Mussolini were strong men in their own right, said Jung, equivalent to tribal chiefs, but Hitler's power, like that of a medicine man, was a magic that derived from his people's projections. Jung went on:

Hitler is the mirror of every German's unconscious. . . . He is the loudspeaker which magnifies the inaudible whispers of the German soul until they can be heard by the German's unconscious ear. . . . Hitler's secret is twofold: first, that his unconscious has exceptional access to his consciousness, and second, that he allows himself to be moved by it. He is like a man who listens intently to a stream of suggestions in a whispered voice from a mysterious source and then *acts upon them*. . . . The true leader is always *led*. . . . It is literally true when he says that whatever he is able to do is only because he has the German people behind him—or, as he sometimes says, because he *is* Germany. So, with his unconscious being the receptacle of the souls of seventy-eight million Germans, he is powerful, and with his *unconscious perception* of the true balance of political forces at home and in the world, he has so far been infallible.[21]

---

[21] "Diagnosing the Dictators," *C. G. Jung Speaking* (Bollingen Series XCVII; Princeton: Princeton University Press, 1977), pp. 115-135.

Looking at him in this light, as the mouthpiece for the unconscious fantasies of a whole nation, we could say that Hitler was an animus-man magnified by millions. He was so extraordinarily destructive because his personal strength in no way matched his visionary gifts. He put his inner voices directly into action, unmediated by human ethical considerations.

The twelve years of the Third Reich culminated in a divided Germany and a divided world. Now, as the Berlin Wall falls, I want to believe that the Hitler era has ended on all levels. However, the realist in me says that most of us have a long way to go to achieve the inner integration implied by the symbol of a unified world. If walls keep coming down and we can no longer find others upon whom we can comfortably project the evil in our own souls, it will have to come home. An integrated world demands that we accept full responsibility for our unconscious selves. Is it really possible to live as rounded, whole human beings? How many are up to this monumental task?

More than a year has gone by since Ruth began to scrutinize her painful past. Much of that time she has been depressed and disoriented, often physically ill. Sickness has helped her learn to say no to immoderate demands from family and friends, who collude with her sometime wish to flee from somber self-examination, asking for time and energy that she needs for herself. Relentlessly saturnine, her dreams have brought no relief.

At last the tide turns. Power loses its ugly grip and for the first time a dream is filled with color and light, humor and self-acceptance. Having penetrated the dark, dense matter of her life, she discovers luminous spheres in the depths of the psyche, glowing fragments of meaning that the ancients called *scintillae,* fiery sparks of soul stuff. This material, said the alchemists, is the light of nature, the image of God within us.[22]

---

[22] See Jung, "On the Nature of the Psyche," *The Structure and Dynamics of the Psyche,* CW 8, pars. 388-389.

In Ruth's words:

"I hear a buzzing sound, low vibrations. It is a sound I have only heard once before, shortly after an injection of ketamine. At first I am afraid of the jagged pieces I disintegrated into during that experience. It is the fear of thinking I will never be able to fit the pieces together again. I hold my breath. I lie in the stillness, willing myself motionless, remembering the paralyzing feeling of the drug. But the pieces are not jagged! They are like marbles. Sparkling. Different colors. The spheres appear to be lighted from within. They are joyous and bright, and I am charmed. I play with them and am tickled by how they play with each other. All equal. All beautiful. All moving. I awaken, delighted and reassured. Affirmed."

6
Examining Jung

Touching evil brings with it the grave peril of succumbing to it. We must, therefore, no longer succumb to anything at all, not even to good. A so-called good to which we succumb loses its ethical character. Not that there is anything bad in it on that score, but to have succumbed to it may breed trouble. Every form of addiction is bad, no matter whether the narcotic be alcohol or morphine or idealism. We must beware of thinking of good and evil as absolute opposites. . . . Nevertheless we have to make ethical decisions. The relativity of "good" and "evil" by no means signifies that these categories are invalid, or do not exist.
　　　　　—Jung, *Memories, Dreams, Reflections.*

"Something smells," said my intuition, getting right down to it.

"Shut up," I said. "Somebody must have made a mistake. In any case, it's not my problem."

Intuition sneered and held its nose. "Mistake!" it mocked.

I had to admit that the insurance check on my desk looked like bad news. I had not seen Ophelia for several months, and she did not owe me any money. In any case, she had always paid me directly and the insurance company reimbursed her. I was tempted to sign the check over to Ophelia and mail it to her, no questions asked. It would save me a lot of trouble. Now that my suspicions were aroused, however, my devilish intuition would keep nudging me with its sharp little elbow until I learned the truth.

Sighing, I picked up the phone. "This is Dr. Dallett," I said to the woman at Puget Health Insurance. "I have one of your checks here, for psychotherapy for Ophelia Cartwright. Can you tell me what dates it covers?"

My work with Ophelia had not come to a satisfactory conclusion. In the weeks before she stopped she had dreamed the same dream, a theme with variations, over and over again, but its meaning remained a mystery. Someone was trying to break into Ophelia's house in the dream. Time and time again, she locked her doors and windows and hid under the covers, terrified.

"Ophelia," I would say, "What is it that you're afraid to look at? What are you hiding from?"

We would go over the hours of her days and nights, searching for moments of fear that might give access to the dream's meaning. She would look at me mutely with her round blue eyes and shake her head. I suggested that she face her assailant in imagination, trying to see or hear who it was and what was wanted. She reported that the adversary would neither speak nor show itself in the light. At last, reluctantly acknowledging defeat, I told Ophelia that we could not go on until she was ready to face the fearsome thing, for neither dreams nor her daily life offered other material for analysis. The source of our work had dried up, and on April 24 we had our last session.

The insurance person returned to the phone. "That check was for May 1 and 8," she said.

"I told you so," smirked intuition.

"Thanks," I said, and slowly hung up the receiver.

The next week I wrote the insurance company: "I am trying to locate a possible error in claims submitted over my signature. Could you please send me a list of all dates and amounts paid to Ophelia Cartwright for psychotherapy?"

After that I called Ophelia. "Look," I said, "I got a check from Puget Health for two sessions for you in May, but we stopped working in April. What's going on?"

At first she was furious. "What's wrong with those people? They were supposed to send the check to *me.*" Then, more calmly, she said, "Oh Lord, I must have forgotten to check the box that says to send it to me." The pause before she went on was almost imperceptible. "I only filled out the form for our last few sessions a couple of weeks ago. I didn't remember the dates so I put down any old thing."

What she said was plausible. She did have a habit of putting off financial matters as long as possible and then making a sloppy job of it. I wanted to believe her. "Well ok," I said, "but I'm going to hang onto the check for a while. I've asked the insurance company to tell me the dates of all your claims."

Her reply was cheerful enough. If she were quaking in her boots she covered it so well that I told myself my suspicions were paranoid. However, when Puget Health replied to my letter, I found that Ophelia had been reimbursed for every session we had had and several that we had not.

Why, I asked myself? What was the point? The amount of money involved was less than $500. It must have been a symbolic act. On the face of it she appeared to be a very good girl, but Ophelia's angry, rebellious side, which she could not bear to face, defiantly lived itself out behind her own back and mine.

The worst of it was my own unwitting collusion. On the first insurance form Ophelia brought me to sign, she claimed a fee that was higher than I actually charge. Although she did not say so, I sensed that she was angry when I refused to go along with the deception. She informed me that her previous therapist had padded the fee to save Ophelia from having to pay anything at all.

"Everybody does it," she said.

Something told me she would not hesitate to alter the claim after I signed it, but I left it in her hands anyway. Laziness or the desire to avoid an unpleasant confrontation led me to sign the forms monthly and give them to her to mail, telling her as clearly as if I had spoken the words that I would pretend the shadow I had seen did not exist. If I was afraid of her fraudulence, how could she look it in the eye? How could she meet the fearsome stranger knocking at her door?

Petty dishonesty is as common in therapy as in life. A woman says she will let me in on a tax scam in lieu of a portion of my fee. A man argues that it would not hurt anyone to misrepresent my fee to his insurance company because it is only an organization, not a person.

Jung disagrees. "In therapy," he says, "ethical values must not be injured on either side if the treatment is to be successful."[23] There are good reasons for it. In Greek mythology, the boatman Charon will, for a fee, transport souls across the river Styx. Anyone who tries to cheat him of his payment is left, as Ophelia was, in a kind of limbo on the near bank, unable to reach the spirit world on the other side. Psychologically, ethical lapses in the arrangements for therapy are like cheating the ferryman. The patient who tries to push on without coming to terms with her shadowy behavior risks activating the psyche's dark, vengeful side. That was Ophelia's predicament. To pay Charon, she would have to own up to what she did and make amends. Only then might her inner ferryman show his benevolent face and guide her safely into the underworld of her unconscious psychology.

The hazardous assumption that patients in psychotherapy can and should be shielded from guilt is widely accepted today. At a recent post-graduate seminar, I heard a therapist speak about an adolescent patient who had murdered both parents. At some point in the discussion she said, "Of course, I don't want him to feel guilty . . . ."

"My God!" I thought. "What are you talking about? The boy *is* guilty and if he doesn't feel it, something is terribly out of kilter." The only adequate therapy in such a case would be to help the youngster face and carry the awful burden of his guilt. Only then, by the grace of God, might he ultimately experience authentic inner forgiveness.

Ethics concerns accepted principles of right and wrong, what is customary according to "the character and spirit of a people."[24] The word *ethic* derives from an Indo-European root *seu-* whose character is as paradoxical as evil itself. *Seu-* refers to the third person reflexive pronoun (e.g., "himself,") but also to the social group as an entity. *Self* comes from this root, as do words having to do with the

---

[23] "A Psychological View of Conscience," *Civilization in Transition,* CW 10, par. 852.
[24] Eric Partridge, *Origins: A Short Etymological Dictionary of Modern English* (New York: Greenwich House, 1983), s.v.

individual's separation from others, like *secede, seclude, secret, separate, solitary* and *solo*. However, derivatives like *sibling, sodality, ethnic,* and *hetaera* refer to relatives, relationship, and the group as a whole. At the root of ethics, then, individual integrity and collective values meet. In the event that they clash, a conflict of duty arises.

Because Jung puts the individual rather than social adaptation at the center of psychological work, people sometimes see Jungian analysis as a license to disregard social or legal sanctions. This can lead to a kind of mass presumption, as I once witnessed, for example, when the participants at a Jungian conference parked their cars in all the "No Parking" zones in the neighborhood. However, Jung himself took his responsibilities to the collective very seriously, and stated clearly that "the possession of individual peculiarities is neither a merit nor, in itself, a valuable gift of nature. It is 'just one of those things,' and it becomes significant only to the degree that consciousness reflects upon it, evaluates it, and subjects it to ethical decision."[25]

For Jung, consciousness is the measure of morality. He emphasizes repeatedly that "to act unconsciously is evil,"[26] and offers an apocryphal saying of Jesus as the standard for a higher ethic: "Man, if thou knowest what thou doest, thou art blessed, but if thou knowest not, thou art accursed, and a transgressor of the law."[27] This is a subtle idea that can easily be misunderstood and misused. Real consciousness does not come easily, and never merely ignores the law. The individual who opposes social or legal sanctions consciously knows he will have to pay a price, for civil disobedience never goes unpunished. Should he escape retribution in the outer world, he will still experience inner suffering akin to that of Prometheus, who defied divine authority by stealing fire from the gods and was thereafter tormented by a vulture or eagle feeding daily on his immortal liver.

---

[25] "Introduction to Toni Wolff's 'Studies in Jungian Psychology,'" *Civilization in Transition,* CW 10, par. 896.

[26] "Answer to Job," *Psychology and Religion,* CW 11, par. 696.

[27] Quoted in "A Psychological Approach to the Trinity," ibid., par. 291.

*

In a dream I must interview a young man to determine whether he is ethical enough to be an analyst. His small, round spectacles and little mustache seem vaguely familiar but I do not quite recognize him. I look at a book to see what questions to ask because I have never before conducted an examination of this sort. Paradoxically, at intervals I ask the man himself if I am asking the right questions, for I know he is an expert in this field.

The dream comes at a time when a candidate in the analyst training program has confessed to an extramarital affair with one of his patients. While I cannot condone Aaron's behavior, it neither surprises nor shocks me. It is only by the grace of God that I myself have never fallen all the way into the same trap. I know how hard it is not to act on the intense sexual attraction the analytic relationship can activate. I also know that living it in the world of ordinary reality subverts the consummation of its spiritual/psychological meaning, behind which lies the drive toward inner unity.

Although it is unethical and illegal for an analyst to exploit the power of his position sexually, it sometimes requires nearly superhuman effort to resist. I remember putting a patient's payment checks in an envelope every week and not cashing them for many months because I wanted so badly to meet him in bed instead of my office. I did not feel I could take his money as my legitimate professional earnings until I was confident that we would not become lovers.

This has not been an issue for me recently, however, and the man in my dream is not Aaron. I keep trying to place the hauntingly familiar face, but its identity is just out of reach. A week later the same man makes a cameo appearance in yet another nighttime drama, motivating me to continue reflecting on his image. When I finally recognize him I burst out laughing. He is the thirty-seven-year-old Carl Jung whose picture, taken in 1912, I have recently seen in the first volume of his published letters. His demeanor is so different from the familiar old man's that I failed to recognize him.

*

My friend Rosemary glared. *"You're* judging Jung's ethics?! What gives you the right to do a thing like that?"

I winced. "I know it's presumptuous, but I had this dream . . ." My hands made placating gestures in the air. "It's not really Jung I'm examining, you know. It's me—*my* Jung—my own relationship to the psyche. Jung's work was something incredible. Monumental. You have to have the right attitude to go as deep into the unconscious as he did. There's not a lot of room for error. If you do it wrong, it can blow up in your face. I've made enough mistakes to know that from experience." I stopped and thought about it for a while. "And another thing . . . Jung *also* made some mistakes. Maybe I need to examine them so I won't have to repeat them."

"You're not Jung!" snapped Rosemary, irrelevantly, I thought. She shifted in her chair and set her feet squarely on the ground.

"That's exactly the point. I want to make my own mistakes, not Jung's. On the other hand . . ." I sighed. How could anything I said do justice to the complexity of the inner world? "There is *something* of Jung in me or he wouldn't show up in my dream. If nothing else he was a human being. Just like me."

"Not like you. Bigger. Much bigger. Great men can get away with things that ordinary people can't."

Something about what she said made me uncomfortable. The pioneering spirit of great men and women often impels them to go beyond old boundaries. In that sense they are outlaws. They have to be exceptionally careful of their ethical ground, or they could easily become criminals.

I said, "Well, you have a point. Greatness does take people beyond established ways of thinking about things. But I don't think Jung would agree that his stature exempted him from the rules that govern ordinary mortals. On the contrary."

"I've heard otherwise," said Rosemary. "From people who know."

It was not hard to guess what she was talking about. In an interview filmed several years earlier I had asked James Kirsch, the founding father of the Los Angeles Jungian community, what he thought about Jung's well-known extramarital relationship with Toni Wolff. He replied that Jung considered himself to be a king, and a king needs more than one wife. The romance was not an affair, said James. Toni was a second wife.[28]

"Rosemary," I said, "James must have gotten it wrong. Jung was only thirty-six years old when he met Toni, and the next decade was a terrible time in his life. For all we know, he might not have come through it at all without Toni's companionship and understanding. Under the circumstances, I can't imagine he saw himself as royalty. All of them—Toni, Jung and his wife Emma—had a horrendous time coming to terms with the whole thing. Maybe he thought it was kingship before he matured, but I just can't believe he would have seen it that way later."

Rosemary sniffed. "How do you know how Jung saw it?"

She had me there. My guesses are my own. Maybe they are true of the historical Jung and maybe they are not. But at the very least, they are certainly true of the Jung who resides in my soul.

At the age of thirty-seven, Jung published the German edition of *Symbols of Transformation,* the book that led to a painful break with Freud, whom he saw as something of a spiritual father. Soon after that he fell into a profound and lengthy introversion. For six or seven years, he grappled with the fantasies and images of the collective unconscious. In retrospect he said that the whole of his prodigious life work flowed from this period. At the time, however, it was a struggle to keep his head above water. He wrote:

> The unconscious contents could have driven me out of my wits. But my family, and the knowledge: I have a medical diploma . . . and five children, I live at 228 Seestrasse in Kusnacht—these were actualities which made demands upon me and proved to me again and again that I really existed, that I was not a blank page whirling about in the winds of the spirit. . . . I aimed, after all, at *this* world and

---

28 "Remembering Jung: James Kirsch," Bosustow Video, C. G. Jung Institute of Southern California, 1990.

this life. . . . I meant to meet its obligations and fulfil its meanings.[29]

Not long before, Jung had begun the analysis of the depressed young woman who was destined to become his guide in the unconscious and his colleague, mistress and friend for the forty years until her death. It was his love for Toni that led to many of his discoveries about the anima. On one hand, Jung is often criticized for the love-triangle in which he lived openly with Toni and his wife Emma. On the other, the arrangement is used to excuse affairs between Jungian analysts and their patients. Both perspectives overlook the fact that Jung fell in love with Toni before he made his major psychological discoveries. I have heard that he said he would not have lived his feeling for her in quite the same way if he had known in 1912 what he later learned about the anima. I cannot vouch for the report's veracity, for it came to me third hand, but I believe it is true in spirit. If he were alive today Jung would doubtless make mistakes, but I imagine they would be different ones, congruent with the level of psychological understanding he took such enormous risks to attain in his actual lifetime.

Jungians, too, can learn from Jung's experience. If we emulate the particulars of his life rather than the spirit of individuation, we will blindly make the same mistakes over and over again, living out patterns that may have been right for Jung but are wrong for us. When the personal idiosyncracies of a great man are amplified by many people acting them out unconsciously, they take on archetypal dimensions and become inhuman. Only by becoming fully conscious of the meaning of Jung's discoveries can we avoid enlarging these fragments of collective Jungian shadow.

As I work on my dream, I gradually become aware that there are some parallels between my life at the time and Jung's life in 1912. Am I living the archetype of Jung, I wonder? I am considerably older than he was then, but I, too, have gone deep into the unconscious

---

[29] *Memories, Dreams, Reflections* (New York: Pantheon, 1961), p. 189.

following a break with colleagues, and am also trying to come to terms with an overwhelming attraction to a person of the opposite sex. Jung's work on the animus gives me a way to understand that my own psyche, not a man, is what has me in its grip. In time I leave the relationship, having realized that it has nothing substantial to offer me in the world of everyday reality.

Unlike Jung, I do not at the time of the dream have daily contact with family, friends, patients or outer-world guide to keep me intact. Jung's work is my only lifeboat. Taking a hint from my dream I peruse his writings for references to ethical issues and the problem of good and evil. I cannot escape the conclusion that he was deeply preoccupied with these matters late in his life. It was then, in his seventies and eighties, that he wrote "Answer to Job," "A Psychological View of Conscience," "Good and Evil in Analytical Psychology," and his two major works about the problem of opposites, *Aion* and *Mysterium Coniunctionis.*

Wondering why these particular problems commanded so large a share of his last fifteen years, I remember Laurens van der Post's report of a late conversation with Jung. The old man was in a dark mood and said he felt that his life's work amounted to nothing. My imagination is caught and I speculate about what might provoke such a feeling. Could it be that the dark underbelly of Jungian psychology was already painfully visible to him? At a much earlier time he had spoken in scathing tones of analysis done badly:

> Immature and incompetent persons who are themselves neurotic and stand with only one foot in reality generally make nothing but nonsense out of analysis. . . . Medicine in the hands of a fool was ever poison and death.[30]

Did it depress him to see the distortions of his method that were inevitable when it was taken up by large numbers of people? A letter I came across later suggests that it did:

---

[30] "The Theory of Psychoanalysis," *Freud and Psychoanalysis,* CW 4, par. 450.

I had to understand that I was unable to make the people see what I am after. I am practically alone. There are a few who understand this and that, but almost nobody sees the whole. . . . I have failed in my foremost task: to open people's eyes to the fact that man has a soul and that there is a buried treasure in the field and that our religion and philosophy are in a lamentable state.[31]

*

Analysis is, on the one hand, a human relationship like any other. At the same time it is a special ceremonial event that confers great authority and responsibility upon the analyst. When the power of the archetypal psyche is projected upon the analyst, the relationship becomes a container for the living spirit. Then the analyst must have his wits about him not to overstep human boundaries. If he succumbs to the exhilarating opportunity to be a little god, he will incarnate depth psychology's charlatan shadow.[32] Using a patient sexually, exploitative friendship, and taking financial advantage are a few of the ways in which this commonly happens.

The primary responsibility for conducting an analytic relationship ethically belongs to the analyst, but if you are a patient you can discourage the abuse of power by retaining your inner authority. A competent analyst needs your cooperation, not passive obedience. She will encourage you to express your doubts and questions about her qualifications and way of working, either answering your questions in a simple, straightforward way or trying to help you understand the inner reasons for doubt or mistrust. If your doubts are so pervasive that the work cannot progress, the competent analyst will refer you to someone else.

In work with dreams and fantasies, it is easy to give too much power not only to the analyst but also to the unconscious. Before I knew anything about Jung, a friend told me that the point of Jungian

---

[31] Quoted in Gerhard Adler, "Aspects of Jung's Personality and Work," *Psychological Perspectives,* Spring, 1975, p. 14.

[32] See my book, *When the Spirits Come Back* (Toronto: Inner City Books, 1988), p. 137.

analysis is to understand your dreams in order to do what they say. For many years I did not realize how wrong she was. It is foolish to give dreams the authority to make decisions, for in themselves they are amoral. As Jung says, "dreams lead astray as much as they exhort."[33] "A dream never says 'you ought' or 'this is the truth.' It presents an image in much the same way as nature allows a plant to grow, and it is up to us to draw conclusions."[34]

The relation between dreams and outer reality is anything but simple. As a rule of thumb, it is best to assume that your dream is an image of a drama going on inside you right now, whose meaning requires great effort to understand. If you think its message is obvious, you are probably wrong. All dreams have inner import for the dreamer, even though some also bring outer-world information to consciousness and/or speak to society as a whole. You almost always need to take their images symbolically, not literally, bearing in mind that the symbolic world of spirit is fully as real as the literal world of matter. It is a bad idea to act on a dream unless you have worked deeply to decipher its significance for you at this time, reconciling its message with what you know consciously. Only through a dialogue between your conscious standpoint and that of the unconscious can you arrive at conclusions that do violence neither to outer reality nor to inner truth. If you are in conflict, it is important to become as conscious as you can of the different perspectives within you, carrying the dilemma until resolution comes in its own, often quite unexpected way.

A middle-aged woman who had fantasies of becoming a famous artist was thinking of leaving her marriage. She dreamed that she was trying to fly, but could not get off the ground because her husband was sitting on her back. Her therapist's response to the dream was to cock an eyebrow at her and say, "Well, Maggie, you know

---

[33] "A Psychological View of Conscience," *Civilization in Transition,* CW 10, par. 835.
[34] "Psychology and Literature," *The Spirit in Man, Art, and Literature,* CW 15, par. 161.

what you have to do." Without further discussion she went home and started divorce proceedings, bringing her conflict to a premature conclusion. It was the beginning of a long flight from reality. Alone in the world she proved unable to take care of herself and finally left the ground completely in a prolonged psychotic episode, lost in fantasies that she did not know how to bring to earth.

The trouble was that Maggie was truly gifted. Hers was the tragedy of the person born with large potentials that for one reason or another cannot be fulfilled. The inner recognition of her capacity made her beat her wings against the outer cage of limitations in which fate had imprisoned her, preventing her from reaching her full stature. Her longing to be famous was a distorted expression of what Hermann Hesse, speaking through his character Hermine in *Steppenwolf,* called homesickness for eternity:

> The pious call it the kingdom of God. I say to myself: all we who ask too much and have a dimension too many could not contrive to live at all if there were not another air to breathe outside the air of this world, if there were not eternity at the back of time; and this is the kingdom of truth. The music of Mozart belongs there and the poetry of your great poets. The saints, too, belong there, who have worked wonders and suffered martyrdom and given a great example to men. But the image of every true act, the strength of every true feeling, belongs to eternity just as much, even though no one knows of it or sees it or records it or hands it down to posterity. . . . Ah, Harry, we have to stumble through so much dirt and humbug before we reach home. And we have no one to guide us. Our only guide is our homesickness.[35]

In her childhood Maggie had been severely abused, physically, emotionally and sexually. As is often the case when a youngster is abused, her only defense was to fly out of her body to escape the pain. Now her creative imagination followed the childhood pattern, functioning neurotically to help her escape from hard reality instead of serving a healthy healing process. Only if she found a way to suf-

---

[35] Quoted by James Wright in his translator's note to *Hermann Hesse: Poems* (New York: Farrar, Straus and Giroux, 1970).

fer her actual life, painful at it was, could her fragmented psyche become whole. Then she might find eternity within, for it is often through acceptance of insurmountable obstacles that we first meet the Self, the archetype that leads the way to wholeness.

Maggie confused creative genius with the Self, unaware that genius cut off from realistic limitation becomes grandiose and one-sided. Peter Schaffer's play "Amadeus" portrays Mozart as a top-heavy genius of this sort, lacking humility, relatedness, or connection to human reality. In Mozart's case, poverty, isolation and an early death brought balance into to what was otherwise a one-sided life.

Whenever a part of the psyche is cut off from the whole, enjoying "independence and absolute power,"[36] it acts like a cancer, running endlessly on its chaotic way without connection to the regulating center that insures the organism's health and balance. Thus, for example, cognition becomes "the devil as aerial spirit and ungodly intellect"[37] when it is dissociated from human feeling or sensory reality. Disconnected from the totality, any aspect of the psyche can fly off and create endless amounts of trouble.

In his own classification of psychological types, Jung identified himself as an introverted thinking type, with intuition as his best auxiliary function.[38] Because I share the peculiarities of this arrangement, I feel qualified to talk about its deficiencies from the inside. For a number of reasons, this particular pattern is virtually a setup for stumbling over collective values.

To begin with, the feeling function is what judges whether something is good or bad. Although the feeling of a thinking type is often profound, it also tends to be primitive, undifferentiated, and unreliable. As for intuition, once it gets to the bottom of something it does not judge what it finds. Because it always sees the potential for

---

[36] *Psychology and Alchemy,* CW 12, par. 88.

[37] Ibid., figure 36.

[38] For an introduction to Jung's system see Daryl Sharp, *Personality Types: Jung's Model of Typology* (Toronto: Inner City Books, 1987).

good to come out of evil, it wants to stand back and watch how events develop without interference. In addition, intuition's capacity to see future possibilities, regardless of the reality of how things are now, reinforces the introverted inclination not to take concrete outer facts entirely seriously.

I believe Jung's typology was responsible for the behavior that has caused his name to be hounded to this day by the preposterous accusation of Nazi sympathies. Although his alarm about the Nazi phenomenon is clear in everything he wrote about it, he did not make a simple, clear, and early public statement of his position.[39] When I examine my own type-related proclivities, I can easily see how Jung could have become so interested in trying to understand and explain the psychology of Nazism that he did not consider what collective common sense might have told him, that he had to protect himself. As a result, I imagine it did not occur to him to proclaim the self-evident fact that what the Nazis were doing was evil. His standpoint as a citizen of a neutral country amplified the characteristics of his type.

In any case, it is rarely easy to be sure whether a thing is more good than evil except with hindsight. What appears good on the surface often comes from bad motives and has bad effects. Last week, for instance, I sat in my office and listened to a mother beg her distressed son to let her help him. In the next breath she informed the young man, who was in his early twenties, what she required in exchange for the financial aid she thrust upon him. Getting rid of his black girlfriend was first on the list. To everyone but the mother it was obvious that the "help" she saw as entirely benevolent was a desperate and shabby attempt to control her son's life.

By the same token, good is often hidden behind what appears to be evil. Jung tells a story from the Koran, in which Moses and his

---

[39] For the facts upon which the allegation is made, see the Appendix in *Civilization in Transition,* CW 10, and Aniela Jaffe, "C. G. Jung and National Socialism," *From the Life and Work of C. G. Jung* (New York: Harper and Row, 1971, pp. 78-98). In addition to these documents, my discussions with several Jewish analysts who were analyzed by Jung during the Nazi time have convinced me that the rumor has no factual basis.

servant Joshua ben Nun meet Khidr, an immortal who symbolizes the Self. Moses asks to follow Khidr. The tale continues with the immortal's response:

> "You will not bear with me, for how should you bear patiently with things you cannot comprehend?"
>
> Moses said: "If Allah wills, you shall find me patient; I shall not in anything disobey you."
>
> He said: "If you are bent on following me, you must ask no questions about anything till I myself speak to you concerning it."
>
> The two set forth, but as soon as they embarked, Moses' companion bored a hole in the bottom of the ship.
>
> "A strange thing you have done!" exclaimed Moses. "Is it to drown her passengers that you have bored a hole in her?"
>
> "Did I not tell you," he replied, "that you would not bear with me?"
>
> "Pardon my forgetfulness," said Moses. "Do not be angry with me on this account."
>
> They journeyed on until they fell in with a certain youth. Moses' companion slew him, and Moses said: "You have killed an innocent man who has done no harm. Surely you have committed a wicked crime."
>
> "Did I not tell you," he replied, "that you would not bear with me?"
>
> Moses said: "If ever I question you again, abandon me; for then I should deserve it."
>
> They travelled on until they came to a certain city. They asked the people for some food, but the people declined to receive them as their guests. There they found a wall on the point of falling down. The other raised it up, and Moses said: "Had you wished, you could have demanded payment for your labours."
>
> "Now the time has arrived when we must part," said the other. "But first I will explain to you those acts of mine which you could not bear with in patience.
>
> "Know that the ship belonged to some poor fishermen. I damaged it because in their rear was a king who was taking every ship by force. As for the youth, his parents both are true believers, and we feared lest he should plague them with his wickedness and unbelief. It was our wish that their Lord should grant them another in his place, a son more righteous and more filial. As for the wall, it belonged to two orphan boys in the city whose father was an honest

man. Beneath it their treasure is buried. Your Lord decreed in His mercy that they should dig out their treasure when they grew to manhood. What I did was not done by caprice. That is the meaning of the things you could not bear with in patience."[40]

Joseph Campbell expressed a similar idea when he pointed out that every act has both good and evil consequences.[41] Such a statement curbs self-righteousness and puts the problem of evil in perspective. It does not imply that evil is good, however, and does not excuse wrongdoing. We have to make judgments as best we can and try to do what is right, even while knowing how limited our consciousness is.

Whenever I thought about Ophelia, I felt ashamed. How could I confront her with what she had done, knowing that my own shortcomings had opened the way for her cheating? After I had stewed about it for a few days, I told Sean what had happened.

"I don't know what to do," I said. "There are so many possibilities. What do you think?"

Because Sean's feeling function is reliable and finely tuned, I have learned to trust his ethical judgments. This time he did not say much, but something about the quality of his listening was enough to make me see what had to be done. The next day found me at my typewriter:

Dear Puget Health Insurance,

Thank you for the list of dates and amounts claimed for psychotherapy for Ophelia Cartwright. Ms. Cartwright was reimbursed for six hours of treatment that did not take place. I am herewith returning your check for $112 and enclosing a list of the dates for which she will have to pay you back. I have advised her that she owes you some money, the exact amount of which I do not know.

---

[40] "Concerning Rebirth," *The Archetypes and the Collective Unconscious,* CW 9i, par. 243.
[41] *Joseph Campbell and the Power of Myth,* with Bill Moyers (New York: Mystic Fire Video, Inc., 1988).

Dear Ophelia,

I find that you claimed insurance reimbursement for six more sessions than we actually had. Since the insurance pays less than the full fee, I don't know how much you will have to return. It would probably be a good idea to call Puget Health and find out. I have let them know about the discrepancy, and am sending back their check for $112.

For me, that ended the whole disagreeable episode, but I often wonder whether Ophelia found the courage to face her adversary. Chances are that I will never know.

By the Light of Polaris

God is not only to be loved, but also to be feared. He fills us with evil as well as with good . . . and because he wants to become man, the uniting of his antinomy must take place in man. This involves man in a new responsibility. He can no longer wriggle out of it on the plea of his littleness and nothingness, for the dark God has . . . given him the power to empty out the apocalyptic vials of wrath on his fellow creatures.

—Jung, "Answer to Job."

When the February, 1971, earthquake hit Los Angeles and put the fear of God into me, I was sitting at my desk thinking about a dream. For some reason I had awakened abnormally early that day, just before dawn. Later, after the largest aftershocks were over, I came out from under the desk and wrote down the dream. Although I did not understand its meaning, I sensed that it was exceptionally important. It had a fateful quality, filling me with a blend of dread and anticipation to which the earthquake added an exclamation point:

"I find two flat, round, pale, translucent fish washed up on the beach. I pick them up and eat them. A little later I begin to feel slightly nauseated and wonder if the fish I ate are making me sick. Then I'm reading a book that has pictures and information about fish of this sort. It names them and says that native people sometimes eat them, but occasionally, when they do, they get sick. The fish and the sickness both have the same name. Translated into English it means 'fright caused by malevolent influences from the earth.' I become convinced that the fish are indeed making me sick and decide to vomit them up, but when I try to, I can't. I will have to digest them or die."

Twenty years later, the process of assimilating the contents of the psyche that comprise those two fish has come to define the shape of my life, the edge on which I live. I have moved north, to a place where "fright caused by malevolent influences from the earth" is a daily occurrence. As I write, winds gusting up to eighty miles an hour have closed the bridge, preventing three of my four afternoon patients from keeping their appointments. Last winter a severe snowstorm decimated my practice. During the summer, exceptionally low tides interfered with scheduled ferry runs. Even though I tremble when the wind blows so hard that the windows in my upstairs living room bend and threaten to break, I am glad to live close to terror, in touch with foul-weather gods as fierce as the ones that watched over my Michigan childhood. Better to bow before inner storminess mirrored in the natural world than to roar through life possessed by it.

The climate of Southern California fosters an inflated notion of the ego's power. When I lived there, the odds were good that neither bad weather nor earthquake would seriously interfere with plans made months or even years in advance. Washington state's Olympic Peninsula is another matter. There nature demands its due. I have learned to love as much as I fear the dark, unpredictable gods that compel me to put my plans aside, implacable powers that can and sometimes do abruptly terminate life. I have slowly come to accept the facts of death and other realities as icy as northern waters, the things in the world and myself that are as they are and cannot be changed.

Ancient peoples believed that the devil dwells in the north. Jeremiah said, "From the north shall an evil wind break forth upon all the inhabitants of the land," while Rhabanus Maurus called the north wind "the harshness of persecution" and "a figure of the old enemy." St. Augustine asked, "Who is that north wind, save him who said: I will set up my seat in the north, I will be like the most High?" and Adam Scotus imagined that a frightful dragon's head in the north was the source of all evil. Paradoxically, the north was also believed to be the home of the highest gods. It was called "the navel of the world and at the same time hell."[42] Thus did the harsh beauty

---

[42] *Aion,* CW 9ii, pars. 156ff.

of northern lands move the mythic imagination toward an unthinkable conclusion: The most sublime and infernal things, the Christ and the Antichrist, live together in the same place.

For me, the northern climate frees long hours in which to meet my unconscious self in dreams, fantasies, and emotions as wild as the wind, bringing me face to face with the raw truth of two unappetizing denizens of the deep, tossed up long ago on a Southern California beach. Slowly they yield up their meaning, revealing the best and the worst, the greatest and least that is in me. This peculiar fish meal, an unorthodox holy communion with roots in the original Last Supper, belongs to the time in which we live. The table is set for everyone who can swallow and digest the contradictory nature of the godhead, not as an intellectual exercise, but by turning inward and coming to terms with primordial aspects of the psyche that we habitually deny, repress, and project on others.

*

In *Aion,* Jung wrote at length about the symbolism of the fish, particularly the paired fish of the astrological sign of Pisces. The Piscean eon began with the birth of Christ. The second fish, the Antichrist, first appeared in folklore before the Reformation, and in 1558 Nostradamus predicted the advent of that "usurper from the north," the Antichrist. Now Pisces is drawing to a close. The sign for the coming age of Aquarius humanizes and unites opposites that are separated in Pisces. In the individual psyche, such a union of opposites emerges from a relationship between conscious and unconscious parts of the personality. Only by accepting the unacceptable, by facing ourselves as we really are instead of as we wish and pretend to be, can we carry evil as well as good within ourselves and help heal the split in the contemporary psyche.

For Jung, the idea that we are moving from one astrological age to another does not imply that heavenly bodies determine human affairs. Rather, it depicts symbolically a psychological fact that defies rational description: The collective image of God, which is so far from consciousness that we project it into the stars, is in a process of transformation. As Jung put it, this is "the right moment for a 'metamorphosis of the gods.' "[43]

Ten months after the fish dream, I had what I can only describe as a vision. I have been reluctant to speak of it because our cultural attitudes pathologize such events and discredit the people to whom they happen. However, a surprising number of perfectly sane individuals have told me about experiences of a visionary nature. I suspect that mildly altered states are far more common than we know, but are usually repressed or kept secret because of the stigma attached to them.

Although by no means confined to such people, visions are most likely to visit spiritually gifted individuals who might have been shamans or religious mystics in other times and cultures. These are the intuitive and creative people in our society, often artists and writers, who live close to what Jung called the collective unconscious, the place in the psyche where the stories of the gods are made. Anyone who can confront a visionary experience consciously, distinguish it from physical reality, reflect upon its inner meaning and perhaps give it artistic form removes it decisively from the realm of pathology.[44]

My own vision came as a precious gift that balanced the excessively rational atmosphere of the psychology graduate program in which I was immersed. I had studied so late that night that I was exhausted. Before going to bed I stood in the doorway of my study, drinking in the cool darkness. Out of the corner of my eye I thought I glimpsed a man standing beside my desk. I was not afraid, only a little surprised, and moved to meet him. Then I saw that no one was there. In time I came to see this event as an annunciation that foreshadowed what was to come.

---

[43] "The Undiscovered Self," *Civilization in Transition,* CW 10, par. 585.

[44] For a more extensive discussion of this theme see my book, *When the Spirits Come Back* (Toronto: Inner City Books, 1988), especially chapters 1, 2 and 8.

I was filled with joy and love, an emotion so intense that I wept. When I went to bed I could not sleep, but lay in a state of ecstasy. I do not remember whether hours passed or only minutes before I saw the image, clearer than a dream although I was wide awake. A young man with long dark hair was walking in the desert. Suddenly he threw himself backward against a large rock, arms flung out, chest to the sky. A knife came down from above and plunged into his chest, and bright red blood flowed in all directions from the wound. At first I was frightened, but curiosity got the better of me and I lay quietly watching the blood flow into the desert sand until the image faded.

Afterward I expected to fall asleep, but more was to come. The faint sound of choral music intruded on my consciousness and I thought a neighbor must be listening to a late-night radio program. I strained to hear, not quite able to make out the words. When I got out of bed and went to the front door, the sound got fainter.

"Heavenly music," I said to myself with a sheepish laugh. The hair on the back of my neck was erect. By now I was wide awake and turned on some lights, but nothing interfered with the mood of deep, deep joy.

Shortly the music stopped, but for months thereafter, at unexpected moments, I would hear the sound of distant music. In time its otherworldly quality convinced me that, like the dream of the two fish, what I had seen and heard did not belong to my personal psychology alone. The tale my psyche told was of a dark, unknown god's voluntary sacrifice to a nameless higher power. His death resembled that of Christ but was different in many respects, particularly the fact that he was alone, with no human agent to serve his passion. It would be many years before I learned his name, but now his very essence and energy flowed into the earth, where it would go on living until it found an appropriate container. At its largest level, I came to see the vision as a snapshot of God-energy in transition, the end of the old eon and the birth of the new.

Like the two fish in my dream, the vision contained profoundly positive possibilities along with monstrous ones. If I took it in the wrong way, too literally or personally, it could become a kind of blood lust, on the one hand, or suicidal self-sacrifice on the other. The dark side of this archetype pervades contemporary life. Because we do not understand and honor its sacred significance, it is responsible for evils like the ritual murders that take place in Satanic cults, the murders instigated by people like Manson and Hitler, the ritual suicides at Jonestown. I believe it also lies behind less dramatic forms of abuse and self-destruction so common in everyday life that we hardly notice them. However, the vision hints that the right kind of sacrifice could redeem this god.

In my memory, the flowing blood of the god eventually merged with the ecstatic feelings of love and joy. I was as if drunk on the god's energy, an intoxication that would remain benevolent only as long as I was fully aware of its spiritual nature. Reverence and awe, gratitude and a healthy amount of fear, might protect me from the dark possibilities in such an influx of divine emotion.

Intoxicate means literally "to put poison (toxin) in." *Toxin* derives from the Greek word for a bow, and refers to the poison put on arrows. The gods Cupid/Eros and Mercurius are both archers whose "darts of passion" are not entirely benevolent. The alchemists saw Mercurius, the elusive, two-faced nature-spirit who embodies the transformative power of the unconscious, as a "poison-dripping dragon" who could bring both "good luck and ruin." The positive aspect of Mercurius, the "light of nature, the light of the moon and the stars" is only available to "those whose reason strives toward the highest light ever received by man."[45] That is, the profoundly activated unconscious brings illumination to anyone who sincerely wants objective knowledge of the Self. This is no small matter, because such knowledge destroys the ego's pleasant illusions about itself. However, when the desire for higher truth is lacking, inner work serves the shadow and Mercurius' poisonous face prevails.

Edinger speaks of the poisonous side of Eros, expressed by

---

[45] All references to Mercurius are from "The Spirit Mercurius," *Alchemical Studies,* CW 13, and *Psychology and Alchemy,* CW 12.

Goethe in "the terrible equation: love = rat poison."[46] Cupid's arrow stirs up a person's most unconscious psychology. To assimilate love's poison, I have to become aware that whatever my lover arouses in me is mine—my passion, fear, passivity, protectiveness, jealousy, nurturance, fury, and frustration; my complexes and child-hood deprivations—all belong to me, even though I may never see them or their effects until I meet the person who triggers them. As long as I believe my lover is the cause of my problems, I will miss my life. He only provides the occasion for me to get to know parts of myself that would otherwise remain unconscious. In this respect, he is like my analyst.

I have noticed that the psyche of any analyst with whom I work affects my dreams in inexplicable ways. When I change analysts, my dreams change, and the place where the two psyches overlap often becomes a primary focus of the work. I do not believe it was a coin-cidence that both the fish dream and the vision came during my anal-ysis with Max Zeller, a gentle, vulnerable man whose poetic soul touched me to the core. I loved him with the gratitude that wells up when places in the psyche long forgotten or never met before are nurtured and given their true value.

Such an emotion is akin to the mystic's love of God. When it comes up in analysis, it deserves to be treated with the utmost care and respect, for behind it lies the largest dimension of the work, a relationship to the living spirit. To belittle it, reducing it to personal factors alone or using the word "transference" in a careless or dis-paraging way, can destroy its immense healing power.

If Max had not been miraculously discharged from concentration camp in 1939, in the nick of time to escape from Nazi Germany, I would never have met him. As I recall the story, his devoted wife Lore pleaded daily for her husband's release until a Nazi official's covert act of kindness suddenly set him free. More than thirty years

---

[46] Edward F. Edinger, *Goethe's* Faust: *Notes for a Jungian Commentary* (Toronto: Inner City Books, 1990), p. 35.

had passed the day that Lore poked her head into the room in their Los Angeles home where I was waiting for my analytic hour. She wanted to introduce me to Max's old friend Johann, whom he had not seen since their student days in Berlin before the war.

The courtly gentleman stood up when I entered the room, bowed from the waist and held out his hand. "Guten tag."

Automatically, I bowed and returned his greeting. "Guten tag. Guten tag, Herr Schmidt."

My head was spinning. Could this be the man in whose house I had lived as an exchange student, long before I ever heard of Max Zeller? It scarcely seemed possible, but several minutes of halting German conversation confirmed that he was indeed the same Johann Schmidt.

My mind went back to the faraway summer when, naive for my eighteen years and only minimally aware of the part Germany had played in the Second World War, I had been with the Schmidt family in Bonn. Herr Schmidt was a charming man, formerly a Nazi and at present a member of the Bundestag. At home he deferred to his wife who ruled the roost with a hand of iron. I stayed out of Frau Schmidt's way as much as possible and spent most of my time with the family's adolescent son and daughter. This was a mistake, for she took my avoidance for guilt and developed a paranoid fantasy that I was stealing the silverware. The forks were found and my name cleared, but a cloud hung over the rest of my visit.

Every morning when I came down for breakfast, I made a stiff little bow to each of the Schmidts in turn, shaking hands and saying briskly, "Guten Tag." Every night before bed the procedure was repeated with the words "Guten Nacht." My body became as familiar with the ritual as with the movements of riding a bicycle or driving a car. Once learned, such patterns are not forgotten.

On balance it was not a pleasant experience. When I returned to college I was glad to put the Schmidts out of my mind. It was a shock to meet the paterfamilias nearly a quarter of a century later, happily drinking tea in the Los Angeles home of my beloved analyst. Was this improbable conjunction merely a coincidence?

"Linked fates," said Max.

"But why?" I wanted to know. "What does it mean?"

Jung gave the name synchronicity to the coincidence of events that cannot be connected by the laws of cause and effect but appear to be linked through a similar meaning or pattern. A synchronistic event between two people is like a little miracle, an epiphany where, for a moment, a god peeks through. I believe it is a sign that the same archetype has been activated in the unconscious of both, drawing the people together as if by a magnet that belies surface differences.

I have struggled for years to grasp the import of that unlikely meeting with Herr Schmidt, convinced that it would help me see deeper into the part of my soul that looked back at me from Max's face. Max died before we could fathom what lay in the unconscious between us. Only now, looking back, can I glimpse some of the patterns woven then. Now I see Wotan peering out of my tapestry, and believe the god of wind and storms must surely have been active in the psyche of my mentor, awakened with a vengeance by his victim role in relation to the Nazis. Indeed, the dark spirit is the subject of one of Max's published papers.[47] I take this as partial confirmation of my guess, even though his essay deals with different incarnations of that deity than the Teutonic lord of the hunt or the Norse shaman who had one blind eye.

Twelve years after Max's death I sat in the office of my ophthalmologist. "The good news," said the doctor, "is that it's not likely to get worse."

Trying to control a growing feeling of belligerence, I reminded myself that Dr. Holmes was not the cause of my darkening eyesight. I kept trying to remember when I had first noticed it. Several years after I moved north to Seal Harbor, I thought, and not too long after I met Sean. Maybe Cupid shot me in the eye. The idea amused me and I smiled, startling Dr. Holmes who was saying, "It won't get

---

[47] Max Zeller, "The Dark Spirit," *The Dream—The Vision of the Night,* 2nd ed. (Boston: Sigo Press, 1989), pp. 42-56.

any better, either. There is a pit in your optic nerve that corresponds exactly to the blind spot we found in the upper right-hand quadrant of your visual field. I could try to repair it with a laser, but it's chancy. Not worth it unless it gets worse."

I stared. *Worse?* Did he have any idea how much it already interfered with my vision? Briskly he gathered his papers together and stood up. "Wait," I said. "What would make a thing like that happen?"

He shrugged. "Who knows? You get older, the body wears out . . ." He seemed to be embarrassed by the mystery of advancing age. It is hard for a doctor not to have answers. Hard for me, too.

I was in the car driving home before I remembered that Wotan/ Odin gave up one of his eyes to drink from Mimir's fountain. Was it Wotan who made a pit in my optic nerve, in the strange, irrational way the psyche has of touching the body? For some reason, the idea made me feel better. If I could understand the meaning behind the hole in my eyesight, the knowledge might be worth the price.

Wotan, a.k.a. Woden and Odin, dwells exclusively in northern lands. A wandering god who unleashes passion and the lust for battle, he presides over war, frenzy, wind and storms. He embodies the untamed spirit in nature as it is in the north, "an irrational psychic factor which acts on the high pressure of civilization like a cyclone and blows it away,"[48] and "whose sole purpose is to arouse life and trouble and strife and misunderstanding."[49] A relative of the devil, Wotan manifests the wild and immoderate instincts and emotions that Christianity has repressed. He eats no food, for wine is all the sustenance he needs and, like the Greek Dionysus, he is intoxicating. Jung likens Wotan to the volatile Mercurius, and says he represents a singularly primitive psychological state "in which man's will was

---

[48] Jung, "Wotan," *Civilization in Transition,* CW 10, par 389.

[49] Jung, *Nietzsche's* Zarathustra: *Notes of the Seminar Given in 1934-1939* (Bollingen Series XCIX), ed. James L. Jarrett (Princeton: Princeton University Press, 1988), p. 898.

almost identical with the god's and entirely at his mercy."[50]

To be identified with God's will is to be overcome by what Edinger calls the greedy, lusting, devouring "primordial concupiscence of being,"[51] seized by a Power that will stop at nothing to satisfy itself. As I write, the Iraqi dictator Saddam Hussein illustrates the point by eating his neighbor Kuwait and threatening to gas anyone who gets in the way. During the Third Reich, the berserk vision of one demented man became horrifying reality when a whole nation identified with God.

It is not necessary to go so far from home for examples, however. I think of Wotan whenever I see a child screaming because she cannot have her way. Parents sometimes project a god-image upon a child, whom they then overindulge and fail to limit appropriately. The overly harsh, sadistic, or unpredictable discipline of a parent who is himself playing God has a similar effect: The child's real needs are not met and she remains raw and angry, even though she may be outwardly compliant. Since no one has ideal parents, most of us are left with something inside that resembles a tyrannical infant, expressing itself in an unconscious demand for people and events to conform to our insatiable expectations.

This part of the psyche is as wild as an animal or the power locked up in the nucleus of the atom. Although it is no more intrinsically malevolent than a blizzard or an earthquake, as long as it is unconscious it can wreak incredible destruction. Many years ago, I was startled when the figure of Jung, addressing me in the inner dialogue of active imagination, said: "Janet, you must never forget that *everyone* has a kernel of madness deep in the psyche." I believe he was referring to the untamed power of which I speak, whose expression we regularly sedate and lock up in mental hospitals. We do not like to go near such monstrous energies in ourselves, nor take responsibility for them, but to do so has its rewards. For one thing, carrying

---

[50] "Wotan," *Civilization in Transition,* CW 10, par. 394.
[51] *Encounter with the Self: A Jungian Commentary on William Blake's* Illustrations of the Book of Job (Toronto: Inner City Books, 1986), p. 55.

our share of the psyche's nuclear power is intrinsically satisfying. For another, doing so gives access to creative resources that lie on the far side of archetypal destructiveness. Thoreau's assertion that "in wildness is the preservation of the world" has meaning far beyond its intent, for the psyche's wildness is a doorway to the Self.

Mythic images of Wotan unbridled are like x-rays of the psychology of abuse. This god is a close relative of the Yahweh who treated Job so disgracefully, for where Job was concerned God "knew no moderation in his emotions and suffered precisely from this lack of moderation. He himself admitted that he was eaten up with rage and jealousy."[52] When Wotan is activated in the unconscious, a trinity of archetypal roles called the rescue triangle[53] tends to come into play. The self-pity and long-suffering accommodation typical of the *victim* role, as well as the invasive attempts to save people from themselves that characterize the role of *rescuer,* violate individual integrity as surely as the sarcasm, ridicule, condescension and overt violence of the *persecutor.* These compulsive patterns, all driven by anger, are virtually epidemic today.

Whenever you do something you do not really want to do for someone else, without adequate compensation, you risk setting the rescue triangle in motion. You may do it because the other person wants you to, or you think he does, in which case your rescue attempt makes you the victim. Or you may victimize the other by insisting that you know better than he does what he needs or wants. The roles go round and round, both between people and within the same person. Whoever is in the victim position today is likely to gather enough strength to play the persecutor tomorrow. All too many family relationships rest on this explosive triangular foundation, beginning with the tacit agreement: "I'll do things I don't want to for you, if you'll do things you don't want to for me." On the international level, the rescue triangle may be a primary cause of war.

---

[52] Jung, "Answer to Job," *Psychology and Religion,* CW 11, par. 560.
[53] Claude Steiner, *Games Alcoholics Play* (New York: Grove Press, 1971), pp. 131-134.

Sacrifice is, of course, a legitimate and often necessary spiritual/psychological act. However, authentic sacrifices for another person are relatively rare. They come from real love, not dependency, are not imposed against the other's will, and do not have strings attached. Made by conscious choice rather than unconscious compulsion, they are not part of the rescue triangle.

The unrealistic cultural prohibitions against selfishness that have grown out of Christianity provide fertile soil for the rescue triangle. We forget that Jesus said, "Love thy neighbor *as thyself.*" Jung has hinted that conscious Christian ideals may be linked to the figure of Wotan in the unconscious.[54] The rescue triangle makes this connection visible, for each of the three roles forms an aspect of the Judeo-Christian archetype: Yahweh is the persecutor and Christ is both victim and savior. To identify unconsciously with divine power, by enacting it in such concrete and literal ways, releases the archetype's dark side, one of whose names is Wotan.

Although his potential for destruction is awesome, Wotan is not all bad. His dual nature as "a god of storm and a god of secret musings"[55] is as contradictory as the paired Piscean fish. On the positive side, Wotan is a god of poetry, wisdom and healing, lord of the runes, sorcerer and prophet. He is as present in poetic inspiration and divine intoxication as in such dark embodiments as lust for battle, fanatical self-righteousness, infantile rage, compulsive sexuality, greed for power, abusive ways of relating, or alcoholism and other forms of addiction.

Wotan is one variant of the dark god whose redemption may well be the central spiritual task of our time. Jung suggests that the Nazi catastrophe marked only the beginning of Wotan's emergence into the contemporary collective psyche: "[He] must, in time, reveal not only the restless, violent, stormy side of his character, but also his

---

54 "The Christian *Weltanschauung,* when reflected in the ocean of the (Germanic) unconscious, logically takes on the features of Wotan." ("The Phenomenology of the Spirit in Fairytales," *The Archetypes and the Collective Unconscious,* CW 9i, par. 442)

55 "Wotan," *Civilization in Transition,* CW 10, par. 384.

ecstatic and mantic qualities—a very different aspect of his nature."[56] He "symbolizes a spiritual movement affecting the whole civilized world,"[57] not just Germany. Indeed, "Wotan is here again"[58] and countless individuals find themselves face to face with the dark power of the god in their own psychology.

How can we carry this dangerous energy constructively, without hurting anyone? Two remarkable episodes in the life of Odin point the way. My discussion will focus on anger and its derivatives, but I believe these stories show how to redeem the power drive and emotional intoxication that are part of possession by any archetype.

Odin's uncle Mimir, "he who thinks," owned the fountain containing all wisdom and knowledge. Odin was so thirsty for its water that he was willing to pay Mimir one of his eyes for the privilege of drinking from it. For this reason, says Jung, Odin/Wotan "is an exceedingly apt symbol for our modern world in which the unconscious really comes to the foreground . . . and forces us to turn one eye inward upon it."[59]

Like the man in my long-ago vision, Odin suffered a Christ-like fate, initiated voluntarily and carried out alone. To rejuvenate himself, he pierced his side with his own spear and hung upside down for nine days and nights on Yggdrasil, the world tree that connects heaven, earth and the underworld. In an ancient poem, the god says that in this ordeal he was "consecrated to Odin, *myself consecrated to myself.*" [60] All the while he carefully watched the earth, hoping that someone would bring him nourishment. No one did, but on the ninth day the runes appeared. When he lifted them up he was released from the tree, and gave the ancient Germanic alphabet and source of occult wisdom to the world.

The stories of Odin's painful self-renewal hint that the dark god

---

56 Ibid., par. 399.

57 *C.G. Jung Letters,* vol. 1, p. 280.

58 Ibid., vol. 2, p. 594.

59 *Nietzsche's* Zarathustra: *Notes of the Seminar,* p. 869.

60 *Larousse Encyclopedia of Mythology* (London: Paul Hamlyn Ltd., 1959), p. 261 (emphasis added).

can be transformed by anyone with the courage and endurance to submit willingly to the agony of emotional storms, while seeking their inner meaning and refraining from taking them out on anyone else. This spiritual undertaking requires a firm footing in heaven and a clear view of hell, a religious attitude that honors the awesome power of psychological energies as overwhelming as nuclear power in the physical world. Odin/Wotan turns the Christian archetype on its head. He does not hang on the tree to save anyone else, but for himself alone, driven by a thirst for self-knowledge and his own redemption. No enemies martyr him, no soldiers pierce his side, for he is consecrated to himself and knows he is the cause of his own pain. In the individual, such solitary acts of sacrifice have far-reaching consequences: They give birth to the enlarged consciousness that just might enable the peoples of the earth to live with each other in the time to come. Surely this gift to humankind is at least as great as the runes.

I want it to be clear that emotion is not what is sacrificed, but rather the acting out of godlike power. It is crucial not to repress or deny emotion, but to endure it until it changes in its own way. Under ordinary circumstances, anger is a healthy instinctive response to physical or psychological injury or threat. When it comes up, it is important to evaluate the situation and take whatever conscious steps you can to protect yourself. Otherwise, the anger is likely to seize you and try to dominate, overwhelm, hurt or destroy the aggressor. If you manage to repress your feelings, they will build up explosive pressure in the unconscious and have their way indirectly, behind your back.

Self-righteousness and the conviction of absolute rightness are some aspects of identification with divine power that can be modified by the suspension between the opposites that Odin's plight implies: "Maybe I'm right, but then again, I could be completely wrong. I imagine what I want to do is good, but I realize that I cannot foresee all the consequences." Human doubt creates enough separation from rage to give a choice about whether, how, and when to express the anger.

Hung as he is with feet reaching toward heaven and an eye fixed on the earth, Odin is focused on life in this world, not the hereafter. With one of his eyes turned inward and the other down, he is in a position to see both himself and others objectively, without illusions. Perhaps the reason for grounding his feet above, in the highest spiritual ideals, lies in the fact that the price of being seized by God's dark power can be high indeed if you do not have your values straight. For instance, Anneliese Aumüller has written about her analysis of a twenty-two-year-old Nazi fighter pilot who could not do his job because he had lost the capacity to differentiate colors. His disability had no physical basis, but psychologically his approach to life was black and white: "Everything that was useful to Germany, Hitler and the victory, was good; everything else was bad." His first dream in analysis depicted his brother dressed in an SS uniform, but "everything was the wrong way. The uniform was white instead of black, and—yes—his face was entirely black." The dreams continued to make the point that the dreamer had things backward, a message he was naturally reluctant to accept. However, doubts began to surface and he decided to see for himself what Hitler was doing. When he visited a concentration camp he came face to face with the appalling consequences of backward values. Then he killed himself. His suicide note to his analyst said: "I believed too long that black was white. Now the many colors of the world won't help me any more."[61]

In Seal Harbor, it was the first Sunday in January. Dogged by wintery weather and exhausted from the last compulsory orgasm of holiday cheer, the town had virtually closed down, and the weatherman said that a storm moving in from Alaska was due to arrive the next day. The prospect of being snowbound, with temperatures in the teens or below, filled me with excitement edged with fear. I had plenty of firewood and two good stoves in which to burn it, but the house was hard to keep warm in even the best of winters.

---

[61] "Jungian Psychology in Wartime Germany," *Spring 1965,* pp. 12-22.

After dinner Sean and I erupted into one of our sudden, incomprehensible arguments, unable to let a small disagreement go before it escalated into a stubborn power struggle. Even while stamping my foot and insisting that I was right, I was ashamed. In the end the monster got the upper hand and tried to pin the whole thing on Sean.

"You started it."

"No *you* did."

"No, don't you remember, it was when *you said* . . . ," and we were off again. In truth, it was neither Sean nor I who started it, but Wotan's storm troopers running amok, wrecking the love and harmony we both consciously wanted.

Still touchy, we walked down town with a foot of space between us and our cold hands in our pockets. I was remembering our first date and the dream I had that night of fleeing before the onrushing lava of an erupting volcano. Afterward I had the flu and spent two weeks in bed, only to learn later that Sean was sick too. Nothing in the tea and gentle conversation we shared that day explained the unconscious afterburn. Only now that we were committed to the relationship was the heat erupting into consciousness. If we could know it for the volcano it was instead of blaming each other for it, and if we could avoid being incinerated by the lava from the center of the earth, maybe we could get to its deeper meaning. The struggle to endure intense emotions without making each other suffer for them gave agonizing reality to the image of Wotan hanging upside down on the world tree, waiting for the mystery of the runes to reveal itself.

The crisp, starry night was alive with anticipation of the promised storm. As we strolled toward the ice cream parlor, raised voices interrupted my reverie.

"Fuck you!" screamed the woman, running toward her car.

The man's angry words were indistinct. He watched her go, then turned and walked rapidly in the opposite direction. Seconds later she ran after him, howling a stream of obscenities. Then or during the push-me pull-you that followed, he hit her. She ran away and he went after her. He walked off and she clung to him. The drama repeated itself over and over, neither able to leave the savage vortex binding them together.

Sean and I looked at each other, embarrassed to see our own contentiousness mirrored in the escalating violence. "Maybe we should do something," I said. "I think it's reached the danger point."

Sean nodded. "We'd better not get in the way. I'll call the police."

We waited for the officer to break up the fight, then went on to our espresso at the ice cream parlor. By the time we finished, the street was as quiet as if the thing had never happened. We walked home hand in hand, like new young lovers, and the next day the storm from Alaska never arrived.

Wotan came into my life at an early age, through a father who was the victim of sudden storms of rage which, though never directed at me, left me with an abiding terror of the dark passions in the human psyche and a drive to get to the bottom of them. Since the god burned Sean in similar ways, it was easy for us to walk in the footsteps of our parents and wage endlessly escalating psychological war, each blaming the other for volcanic eruptions that we both hated. When I began to realize that my fear of Sean's anger belongs to me, not him, I dreamed that I visited my childhood home. Most of the yard was green and beautiful, but the grass near the faucet was badly scorched because my father, a gardener, had neglected to water it. I put the sprinkler where it would soak the parched grass, and tenderly kissed my father good-bye.

While I was thinking about this dream, the telephone rang. The woman on the line was so upset that she was nearly incoherent. Gradually I understood that she was looking for a therapist for her seventeen-year-old daughter, who had beaten up her boyfriend and broken every window in the house the night before. Although I do not ordinarily work with teenagers, the synchronicity was so striking that I gave the girl an appointment the same day. Perhaps we had something to teach each other.

Sobbing, Lisa told me she felt that something was terribly wrong with her. "I can't control myself," she said. "but I don't *want* to hurt

Robbie. I love him more than anyone in the world."

"What made you so mad?"

"I don't know. It was nothing. Some stupid thing he said. He didn't mean anything by it. I just couldn't stop hitting him."

Human beings are like that, I told her. We hurt the people we love because they are the ones who get close enough to touch old wounds, sore spots that might otherwise stay hidden. Then the instinct to defend ourselves comes up and we strike out, wanting to hurt the other person back.

"Nothing is wrong with you Lisa," I said. "You have a good, healthy self-protective instinct. But you do overreact. I wonder why?"

The relevant facts soon came out. Although Lisa belonged to what is generally regarded as a "good family," her alcoholic father was subject to fits of rage and violence. When she was ten, he beat her so severely that the state put her in the first of a series of foster homes, where she suffered varying degrees and kinds of abuse, from ridicule and invasion of her privacy to overt violence and sexual harassment. Now she was more or less on her own, but financial dependence tied her to her original family and she continued to be "the bad one," the scapegoat for the abuse patterns in the family closet.

On the one hand, Lisa was not fully aware that she had been abused, and halfway believed that she deserved what had happened to her. On the other, something resembling Wotan in her unconscious was hypersensitive to every violation of her dignity, however subtle, and rushed to defend her. Once in the grip of the god, she reacted with violence to the small, inadvertent hurts that her boyfriend, who truly loved her, could not help inflicting.

Lisa was a quick study. Young enough to absorb new ideas like a sponge, she had the intelligence and insight to apply some sophisticated concepts to herself. She soon understood that while it is wrong to hurt another person, it is just as wrong to let yourself be injured if there is something you can do to protect yourself. Once she saw that she could not help raging as long as rage was her only defense, she guarded her self-respect more consciously. She acknowledged deep wants and feelings, long denied, and moved toward goals she yearned to reach but had never believed she deserved. Whenever she felt belittled, she tried to speak up for herself, moving beyond the inner and outer voices that told her she was no good.

Sometimes the fury of the god rose up in spite of her best efforts. Then she knew she must sacrifice action lest she inflict on someone else the violence that had been done to her. Acknowledging her warlike feelings, she would go off by herself and vent the storm alone in harmless ways.

Lisa did not show up for her ninth appointment. I was startled, for she had never before missed an hour without canceling it well ahead of time. A few days later she called to apologize for forgetting, but the incident set me to thinking, and when she came for her next session I had a question for her.

"Sometimes," I said, "the unconscious makes a person forget her appointment for a reason. You've done a lot of good work in a short time. Have you had any feeling that you might want to stop coming for therapy?"

The relief that flooded her face was my answer. "Yes," she said. "I haven't gotten out of control for a long time, and there's nothing else I want to talk to you about. I know what I have to do now. You can't do it for me. It's up to me."

When I nodded my agreement she went on in a rush. "The main thing is that my Dad is paying for it and—it doesn't make sense— you know what I mean?—to take money from him when . . ." Her voice trailed off, but I did know what she meant because I had been thinking about the dilemma myself. Money can be a deadly instrument of coercion. Until Lisa sacrificed the last shred of financial dependence, it could keep her trapped in the family psychology she was otherwise ready to leave. Delighted that she had understood this without my help, I said goodbye to her.

It was hard for her to see it that way, but Lisa was the lucky one in her family. Painful as it was to be the black sheep, not being able to cover up her problems gave impetus to growth and self-awareness that the others lacked. At seventeen, she had already reached a rare level of psychological honesty, objectivity and insight, enabling her to make major changes in a remarkably short time. When she is older she may want more therapy, but for now she is on her way. Perhaps she is one of a new breed, a rising star of the Aquarian Age. If so, sometime in the next millennium, inner truth may become more important than looking good.

"Have you ever thought," asks Sean, "what a miracle it is that there happens to be a star almost exactly over the North Pole? Without it, sailors might never have learned to navigate. Look at it, all alone up there. Nothing else is anywhere near it." Hunching down to get the angle right, he points to guide my line of sight until my imperfect vision can discern Polaris in the night sky.

"No," I have to admit, "that's something I've never thought about before."

I think about it now, though. If north is where all the opposites in the psyche can come together into a unified whole, then what is the role of the North Star? I am not surprised to find that the alchemists thought about it too. Speaking in their mysterious, dreamlike language they said, "In the Pole is the heart of Mercurius, who is the true fire, wherein his master rests. When navigating over this great sea . . . he sets his course by the aspect of the North Star."[62]

Remembering the hot lava that comes up between Sean and me, I hope our fire is the true fire, the heart of Mercurius, not something false. I imagine the test of its truth will lie in its ultimate effect. If we both survive the fire, we will know our love was true.

One time we got up together at 4.00 a.m. to look at the awesome disk of the moon in coppery eclipse, mirroring the shadow of the earth. If there can be logic in love, I imagine the reason I love Sean is because he cares about things like that, things you only realize are important when you stand still long enough to think about them. When you get right down to it, they are the same things I care about, but we see them from different angles.

---

[62] Quoted in *Psychology and Alchemy*, CW 12, par. 265.

"As above, so below," said the ancients. What goes on in the cosmos reverberates in the little human world and again in the individual psyche. Or is it the other way around? In any case, if you think the connection goes through the air or just happens by magic, you have a surprise coming. Shamans all over the planet know that the center of the universe, the North Pole, is the *axis mundi* that joins the upper and lower worlds to ours, just like Yggdrasil, the world tree. That is where the North Star comes in. It makes the hole. You know, so you can get through to the upper world. In olden times, everybody's house had a central pillar and an opening to the sky, because all human dwellings mirror the center of the universe. And remember, somewhere inside, you have the whole thing too: a pair of fish, Wotan, the pole, a volcano, and even the North Star.

Studies in Jungian Psychology
by Jungian Analysts

Sewn Paperbacks

New, recent and choice:

The Scapegoat Complex: Toward a Mythology of Shadow and Guilt.
Sylvia Brinton Perera (New York). ISBN 0-919123-22-8. 128 pp. $14

Addiction to Perfection: The Still Unravished Bride.
Marion Woodman (Toronto). ISBN 0-919123-11-2. Illustrated. 208 pp. $17

The Creation of Consciousness: Jung's Myth for Modern Man.
Edward F. Edinger, M.D. (Los Angeles). ISBN 0-919123-13-9. Illustrated. 128 pp. $14

The Illness That We Are: A Jungian Critique of Christianity.
John P. Dourley (Ottawa). ISBN 0-919123-16-3. 128 pp. $14

Alchemy: An Introduction to the Symbolism and the Psychology.
Marie-Louise von Franz (Zurich). ISBN 0-919123-04-X. 84 illustrations. 288 pp. $18

The Pregnant Virgin: A Process of Psychological Transformation.
Marion Woodman (Toronto). ISBN 0-919123-20-1. Illustrated. 208 pp. $17

The Jungian Experience: Analysis and Individuation.
James A. Hall, M.D. (Dallas). ISBN 0-919123-25-2. 176 pp. $16

Phallos: Sacred Image of the Masculine.
Eugene Monick (Scranton/New York). ISBN 0-919123-26-0. 30 illustrations. 144 pp. $15

The Christian Archetype: A Jungian Commentary on the Life of Christ.
Edward F. Edinger, M.D. (Los Angeles). ISBN 0-919123-27-9. Illustrated. 144 pp. $15

Personality Types: Jung's Model of Typology.
Daryl Sharp (Toronto). ISBN 0-919123-30-9. Diagrams. 128 pp. $14

The Psychological Meaning of Redemption Motifs in Fairytales.
Marie-Louise von Franz (Zurich). ISBN 0-919123-01-5. 128 pp. $14

The Sacred Prostitute: Eternal Aspect of the Feminine.
Nancy Qualls-Corbett (Birmingham). ISBN 0-919123-31-7. Illustrated. 176 pp. $16

The Survival Papers: Anatomy of a Midlife Crisis.
Daryl Sharp (Toronto). ISBN 0-919123-34-1. 160 pp. $15

The Cassandra Complex: Living with Disbelief.
Laurie Layton Schapira (New York). ISBN 0-919123-35-X. Illustrated. 160 pp. $15

The Ravaged Bridegroom: Masculinity in Women.
Marion Woodman (Toronto). ISBN 0-919123-42-2. Illustrated. 224 pp. $18

Liberating the Heart: Spirituality and Jungian Psychology.
Lawrence W. Jaffe (Los Angeles). ISBN 0-919123-43-0. 176 pp. $16

The Dream Story.
Donald Broadribb (W. Australia). ISBN 0-919123-45-7. 256pp. $18

The Rainbow Serpent: Bridge to Consciousness.
Robert L. Gardner (Toronto). ISBN 0-919123-46-5. Illustrated. 128 pp. $15

Circle of Care: Clinical Issues in Jungian Psychology.
Warren Steinberg (New York). ISBN 0-919123-47-3. 160 pp. $16

Jung Lexicon: A Primer of Terms & Concepts.
Daryl Sharp (Toronto). ISBN 0-919123-48-1. Diagrams. 160 pp. $16

Prices and payment (check or money order) in $U.S. (in Canada, $Cdn)
Add Postage/Handling: 1-2 books, $2; 3-4 books, $4; 5-8 books, $7

Complete Catalogue and SAMPLER free on request

INNER CITY BOOKS
Box 1271, Station Q, Toronto, Canada M4T 2P4
Tel. (416) 927-0355